THE MIDDLE CLASS IN COLONIAL MALABAR

THE MIDDLE CLASS IN COLONIAL MALABAR

A Social History

SREEJITH K.

MANOHAR
2026

First published 2021
Reprinted 2026

ISBN 978-93-90729-59-3

Published by
Ajay Kumar Jain *for*
Manohar Publishers & Distributors
4753/23 Ansari Road, Daryaganj
New Delhi 110002

Typeset by
Ravi Shanker
Delhi 110095

Printed at
Replika Press Pvt. Ltd.

Contents

Acknowledgements

This volume deals with the social history of the middle class in colonial Malabar. And, while doing so, keeping theoretical abstractions to the bare minimum, it explores the lived experiences of people who constituted the middle class and what they made of the changes rapidly evolving around them.

I hail from Malabar, and did my schooling from Tellicherry, one of the principal towns in the region before shifting to Kozhikode, the district headquarters during the colonial period. My father, like some characters in this book, went to Madras for his higher education, after which, returning to Malabar, he served in various colleges, for the most part, at Brennen College, one of the oldest educational institutions in this part of the world. Thus, hailing from Malabar and belonging to a middle-class family, the topic of research has held an abiding interest to me over the years. The book took a long time in its making partly because, after getting a job in West Bengal when the work was only half-done, Malabar had become physically so remote. However, biannual visits to Kerala kept the research going. And, now when finally, as the book is sent off to press, there is a strong sense of relief.

The volume of course is based on my PhD thesis. While the work was in progress, I received help from various people. I take this opportunity to thank them all.

I am deeply indebted to Prof. K.N. Panikkar, who guided me through various stages of writing this work. Prof. Kunal Chakravarty was extremely helpful in seeing me through the formalities required for re-registration. I could not have had a better co-guide than the late Prof. M.S.S. Pandian, whose informal ways helped one tide over the tension of the last few days before submission.

I remember on this occasion Prof. P.P. Sudhakaran, whose wonderful lectures on historical methodology at Govt. Arts and Science College, Calicut got one seriously interested in the subject. Thanks are also due to Prof. M.G.S. Narayanan and Prof. P. Venu who were never hesitant in sharing books as well as ideas.

Friends in the same profession like M.R. Manmadhan and M.C. Vasisht helped in locating sources. Debates with fellow-researchers from JNU – Raziuddin Aquil, Kadakkal Ashraf, K.G. Pradeep, Madampat Shajahan and Gilbert Sebastian in particular – helped in formulating ideas and sharpening them. Friends in Bengal like Simonti Sen, Parimal Bhattacharya, Pranabes Bhattacharya and Pradip Chattopadhyay helped me gain insight into the ways of the Bengali *bhadralok*. Suman Nath inspired me to convert the thesis into a book, and meticulously went through the drafts, offering invaluable suggestions in the process.

Over the years, apart from the library at JNU, I have visited several libraries and archives across India – NMML, Sahitya Akademi, and National Archives in Delhi, Connemara Library, the Adyar Library run by the Theosophical Society and Tamil Nadu State Archives in Madras, Kerala Sahitya Akademi and Appan Thampuran Library in Trichur, Mahatma Gandhi Memorial Library in Paral, Deshaposhini Library, Calicut University Library and Regional Archives in Calicut. I thank the staff of these institutions for providing help during my research.

Ammachi, Aroon, Anand and Priya have been a constant source of support all along. My daughter, Brishti, was born after the work was started. Playing with her often provided an escape from the harsh world of research. Urmita was a wonderful companion throughout.

My thanks to all at Manohar Publishers, especially Ramesh Jain and Siddarth Chowdhury, for making a dream come true.

I dedicate this work to the memory of my father and my father-in-law, both of whom passed away while this work was in progress.

SREEJITH K.

INTRODUCTION

The Middle Class
The Context and the Contours

In 1975 the historian Arnie J. Mayer, while lamenting that academics, over time, have not done research on the middle class even as they write prolifically on the working and peasant classes, wondered whether it was due to the fact that social scientists are hesitant to expose the aspirations, lifestyle, and world view of the social class in which so many of them originate and from which they seek escape.[1] This was the period when the Indian academia as well, dominated as it was, by Marxists of various persuasions, exhibited a similar reluctance in exploring the history of the Indian middle class. Since then, however, a large body of work on the middle class has come forth both nationally and internationally. Regional studies have enriched our knowledge about this class which came into their own during the colonial period. However, except for the odd writings on some aspects of its history, a comprehensive work on the middle class in colonial Malabar is yet to appear. This work tries to fill the gap partially in so far as it attempts to explore its social history in Malabar during the late nineteenth and early twentieth centuries. In doing so, political and religious dimensions, on which there have been numerous studies, have been excluded.[2] The year 1871, when the first Census appeared, has been taken as the starting point with the account coming to a close in 1947, when the nation gained its Independence.

Defining the Middle Class

The term middle class was used from around the mid-eighteenth century to describe those people below the aristocracy but above the workers. It is indeed a broad category, and different scholars, over the years have given varying definitions on the subject. Classical Marxism is of not much use in understanding the history of the middle class. Marx did not elaborate on the white-collar class comprising office workers, supervisors, technicians and innumerable others who are essentially a product of capitalist development. He did not anticipate the emergence of a welfare state within a capitalist society, and the consequent growth of an employee class providing the many welfare services such as education, public health, railways, road transport, post and telegraph as well as the growth of a bureaucracy overseeing them. Nor did he anticipate the emergence of a managerial class which forms an important element in the modern capitalist development. For Marx, the middle class had only a limited significance due to it being, in his view, a transient group with a minimal role in the revolutionary process. But that has not prevented a range of Marxist historians, over the years, from writing on the subject. And while doing so, not unlike the sociologists, they have sometimes resorted to non-economic criteria in defining the middle class.[3] While writing on the middle class in England, Eric Hobsbawm observes that upto 1880, the middle class shared the following characteristics: they did not, except as leisure, perform manual labour: paid work prevented their women from becoming a lady; they have to possess some capital or property, however modest; they must employ others for wages at least as domestic servants; they would not be employed for service except by the state or church.[4]

To belong to a middle class, as the term suggests, there must be a class or classes above it as well as below it so that it stands in the middle. Thus, differentiating themselves from a decaying aristocracy above them, and the lower classes below them became crucial in the self-fashioning of the new middle class. According to Hobsbawm, while in the early nineteenth century, the English middle class had identified itself and its values in the first instance against the landed aristocracy and its system, at the end of the century, it did so by stressing its separation from the proletariat which was obviously much easier than acceptance by higher strata.[5] There cannot be strict demarcation between the classes, especially at the extreme ends. As a couple of scholars who worked on the middle class in

England put it, 'In terms of income and labour, the petit bourgeoisie shaded into the skilled working class, [while] on the basis of their ownership of property and a style of respectability, they approached the more substantial bourgeoisie . . .' the petit bourgeoisie, thus, is 'a world in movement'.[6]

Traditional sociological indicators of income and occupation, thus, cannot take us very far in understanding the social category of the middle class. Following the impact of post-structuralism and the 'linguistic turn' in history, some historians have given up on the idea of class as an objective reality. Patrick Joyce, for instance, focuses on the study of the language that people used, since, for him, it was the words they employed that provided the essential source of their social and political identities. Thus conceived, class was neither an objective guide to social reality nor a shared subjective experience. Classes never actually existed as recognizable historical phenomena, still less as the prime motor of historical change. They were nothing more than rhetorical constructions, the inner imaginative worlds of every man and every woman, seeking as best as they could to explain their social universe to themselves.[7] Similarly, Dror Wahrman has argued that more than a socio-economic reality, the 'middle class' was a product of language in political discourse.[8] There are still others who take a middle position on the question of class. For David Cannadine, 'it is somewhere between the over-determined reductionism of Marxist analysis and the free-floating subjectivities of the historians of language that we should seek to discover, describe and discuss class as it has actually existed and developed in Britain during the last three hundred years'.[9]

Recent writings on the middle class have tried to address the gendered nature of middle class consciousness. Catherine Hall, for instance, argues that the men and women of the middle class adopted distinct class identities and that the language of class formation was gendered.[10] Male apprehensions regarding women's economic, social and intellectual potential ensured that the latter will not have any voice in the body politic. The acquisition of gendered subjectivity, according to Catherine Hall, was a life-long process in which linguistic, cultural and symbolic representations of sexual differences played a vital part as did social organization.

In India, at the end of the nineteenth century, Surendranath Banerjea gave currency to the concept of a 'new middle class' which, according to him, was created by the impact on Indian society of Western culture, the carrier of 'enlightenment, freedom, progress and prosperity'.[11] Since then, several others have reflected on this group. However, there is no unanimity among scholars on what constitutes the 'middle class'. Like elsewhere, not being directly linked to the means of production – unlike the workers and the bourgeoisie – it has not been the easiest of tasks to identify, let alone, define them. Indian society in the late colonial period was extremely complex, heterogeneous and segmented. Michelguglielmo Torri observes that 'the usual contradictions to be observed in any society in which capitalism is gradually emerging as the dominant mode of production, were compounded by divisions arising from castal, religious and linguistic factors'.[12] All discussions on class in India inevitably leads to the problem of caste. As B.N. Ganguli says, 'any attempt to conceptualise the Indian middle class, difficult in itself, is rendered more difficult by the dimension of "caste" which introduces different principles of social stratification. An unequal caste society has a kind of stratification that does not necessarily coincide with a purely economic stratification.'[13] And, as Sumit Sarkar has shown us in the case of the *bhadralok* in colonial Bengal, the middle class was not a homogeneous group, but was constituted by different layers positioned at varying levels of affluence and influence.[14]

In a way, it is in what they were 'not' that we can identify the middle class. Regarding the Bengali *bhadralok*/middle class, Rajat Kanta Ray writes that 'in their own perception, this was a "middle class-bhadralok" world which situated itself below the aristocracy, but above the lesser folk engaged in manual labour and generally from the lower castes, or the Muslims'. According to him, this intermediate strata, 'identified neither with a propertied class owning the means of production, nor with a propertyless class living by physical labour and did not have any definite class alignment'.[15] For, Sumanta Banerjee, the lifestyle and appearances demarcated the middle class from the rest. He says that 'the outward manifestation of the *bhadralok* which were made possible by a basic standard of income were residence in a "pucca" house, attention to one's sartorial style in public, use of a chaste Bengali that was being shaped from the middle of the nineteenth century, and a noticeable knowledge of English language and manners.'[16] In short, as Sanjoy Joshi says, 'being middle class was basically a project of self-fashioning in the realm of the public sphere, a process which was in the making, and not something already given'.[17]

To sum up, income alone will not suffice to define the middle class even though a salary which would provide enough for some savings is a prerequisite. That apart, men should not be involved in manual labour while their women should be staying at home and looking after the household even though, at a later stage, they would be allowed to involve themselves with what was described as feminine work which included nursing and teaching. A *pucca* house is a must, so was a level of education which would be raised as the years went by. Social networks and keeping up with the cultural fashions of the day added to the image of the middle class. Those described as the middle class in the following pages would have fulfilled most of the above criteria.

Malabar: The Context

Malabar, in ancient writings, denoted the whole of Kerala. In the British period, it referred (as this volume does) to the territory between Cochin in the south and Canara in the north, lying between the Arabian Sea on the west and Western Ghats in the east, consisting presently of the districts of Kasargod, Canannore, Kozhikode, Malappuram, Wynad and Palghat. The area had come under British rule in 1792 with the Treaty of Srirangapatanam on 18 March 1792 at the end of the Third Anglo-Mysore war.[18] Malabar, during the colonial period, though culturally similar and having linkages with the rest of Kerala, was administratively part of Madras presidency and unlike the princely states of Travancore and Cochin, directly under British administration. It was only in 1956, with the re-organization of states in independent India, that it became part of the newly-created Kerala State. Prior to its reorganization in 1956, the area of the district was 5,802 sq. miles, and the population according to the 1951 census was 4,758,000. With a density of 820 persons per sq. mile, it was one of the most densely populated districts in the Indian union. There had been a steady increase in population during the late nineteenth and early twentieth centuries. According to the earliest comprehensive census in 1871, the total population was 2,260,000, while the next one in 1881 showed 2,365,000. Though the first one is not considered reliable owing to enumeration irregularities, it is clear that political stability, freedom from wars and control of epidemics had led to an increase in population in the subsequent years. By 1941, the total population of the district had risen to 3,929,000, of which the low-caste Hindus constituted 48 per cent, Muslims comprised 30 per cent, while high caste Hindus made up 20 per cent, and the Christians around 2 per cent.[19] The demography of Malabar, however, did not remain static over the years. From 31,191 in 1931, the Christian population in the region increased to 4,42,510 by 1971.[20] Missionary activities may have played a part, but the main reason was Christian migration into Malabar from the south where land was in short supply. The process began as a trickle in the 1920s at places like Mannaarghat and Kuttiadi, and after the Second World War, intensified. The consequences were immense. Many adivasis got alienated from their lands, and large tracts of land, hitherto uncultivated, including forests lands were brought under the plough, and more cash crops including ginger and rubber were introduced in the region.

The debate has not died down as to when and where modernity emerged first. Most assume it was in Western Europe in the post-Enligtenment period, and then slowly diffused to the rest of the world. This line of argument, at most times, refuses to take into consideration the influence of the orient in moulding European modernity. Plus, in the case of Malabar, it has to be remembered that long before the advent of Europeans here, the people on the west coast, especially traders, had strong relations with Arabs and others. Thus, it is clear that there cannot be a uniform, universal model of modernity for the whole world. However, there is no doubt that colonial rule brought about dramatic changes in the society of Malabar.

British rule and the institutions they created destroyed the political, material and ideological basis of the erstwhile ruling classes in Malabar even as evangelical and utilitarian critiques constantly undermined the legitimacy of the moral and cultural order supported by them. Modernization of society, though aborted in the colonial context, became a reality through, among other things, the ending of institutions like slavery and *Marumakkathayam*. As the feudal order gave way to a colonial capitalist economy, the Nair militia was disarmed, the powers of the caste and religious institutions curtailed, and a bureaucracy not dependent on the feudal lords created. Earlier, government service had been considered as personal service to king. Now, public service became impersonalized, and contractual in nature with written service conditions and monthly salary. To acquire it, education and training became compulsory.[21] During the late nineteenth century, especially during the viceroyalty of Ripon, when self-government began to be experimented with, Indians got absorbed into the administration. Thus was created the circumstances favouring the emergence of a socially and politically significant middle class.

Unlike in the West, in India, under colonial conditions, a stunted capitalism did not give rise to a prominent industrial bourgeoisie. Colonialism gave no emphasis to technological and industrial development, and the new system of education gave no importance to vocational training, and, instead, only trained 'writers'. Following the growth of a colonial bureaucracy and a service sector, the middle class here was constituted by urban professionals and the bureaucrats. Add to that the intelligentsia who were to play a pivotal role in the emerging public sphere, and we get a picture of the new middle class in colonial India. Though being an intellectual was not a prerequisite for becoming a member of the middle class, intellectuals were an important constituent of this group. It is, infact, partly through the voices of the likes of O. Chandu Menon, an important functionary in the judiciary, Murkoth Kumaran and Sanjayan, teachers in school and college respectively, as well as those who were professional journalists like K. Madhavan Nair, who, through their active presence in the public sphere, set the cultural agenda for the region in the early twentieth century, that we shall try to reconstruct the social life of the middle class in colonial Malabar.

Malabar had lagged behind economically during the colonial period, both when, initially, it was a district of the geographically distant Bombay presidency, and when later it became part of the Madras presidency, whose authorities always seemed to give priority to the development of the eastern coast. The British, who saw that, for running the administration, revenue from trade and agriculture would suffice, did not bring about any radical changes in production relations.[22] Unlike Travancore, in Malabar, there was only a minimal commercialization of crops, and, consequently, a rich agrarian class who had the required capital to invest in industries, did not emerge. A sound agrarian base for proper industrialization was missing. Industrialization in colonial Malabar, thus, had a stunted growth. An outline of its early history now follows.

The earliest foreign capital invested in the region had been in spice plantations begun in the early nineteenth century by Murdoch Brown in Anjarakandy near Tellicherry. With the demise of Pazhassi Raja, Wynad came under the control of the British, after which several coffee plantations were started there. In the late nineteenth century, British investments were made in the cool, well-watered Western Ghats which were close to ocean transport lanes. This region was ideal for tea and rubber plantations. Robert H. Pierce and Patrick Leslie started in 1862 at Calicut, a coffee processing unit of the products arriving from Wynad. In 1914, the British had started the Kerala Soap Institute, which, in the course of the war, developed into a soap producing unit, and later on produced shark liver oil as well.[23]

For the limited industrial growth in Malabar during the nineteenth century, a major credit goes to the German Basel Mission. Arriving in Malabar in 1834, it incorporated industrial activities along with its missionary work, and initiatives in education and health. It was the pioneer in setting up industries in Malabar, as well as modernizing the existing agriculture and crafts. From 1834 to 1914, it set up modern centres for weaving and tile making, both of which had existed earlier as traditional crafts. Printing and book binding as well as operation of a mechanical engineering establishment were the other industrial activities of the Basel Mission. As Jayaprakash Raghaviah observes, in these enterprises, the workforce was provided by a 'casteless group of converts'.[24] The social engineering initiated by the Basel Mission ensured social mobility for the lower castes including the Thiyyas and Cherumas. At the end of the First World War in 1919, the British government took over Basel Mission's industrial units in India, and placed them under the Commonwealth Trust Company.

By becoming part of the British bureaucracy, and through participation in British trade, a number of natives who had become wealthy and were in a position to invest in industries had emerged by the end of the nineteenth century. In 1884, District Judge, F.H. Wilkinson inaugurated Thiruvannur Cotton Mill, the first locally owned industry with modern management techniques. A.K.T.K.M. Narayanan Nambuthiri, Kalyanji Sundarji, A.L.A.R. Ramaswamy Chettiar, Vrindavan Das and Purushottam Das were the main shareholders. Other native initiatives soon followed in and around Calicut. P. Raman started in 1909, Puthiyara Tile Works, while in 1938, Sait Nagjee Purushottam started the Vegetable Soap Factory.[25] Alongside the businessmen associated with the growth of manufacturing, the period saw an increased number of small entrepreneurs, shopkeepers and merchants who undertook to transport and retail the fruits of industry. There was, consequently, the proliferation of commerce and finance – banks and insurance companies cropped up, including local ventures like Nedungadi bank set up in 1899 at Calicut by T.M. Appu Nedungadi. Other similar enterprises include Maviladath Kumaran's Bharat Bank and City Bank started by Mithavadi Krishnan. The Bank of Madras established its branch at Calicut in 1864. It would later merge with the Imperial Bank of India, and, post-Independence, become the State Bank of India. The expanding economy needed clerks, managers and salaried professionals for which there was no shortage. For the young men of Nair *tarawads*, disgruntled with their state of dependence within the household and the meagre salaries provided by government jobs, joining business ventures of this kind as their managerial staff would have been a lucrative prospect.[26]

Notwithstanding the above examples, native bourgeoisie remained weak both qualitatively and quantitatively through the colonial period. Those who had the ambition did not have the resources, and those who had the resources, did not have the will. As an anonymous writer in a college magazine put it '. . . the numerical strength of graduates in Malabar does not encourage us to be optimistic. Most of them belong to the middle class whose resources would hardly permit them to establish big commercial concerns . . . [and the] aristocratic classes of Malabar . . . are extremely nervous of investing their wealth in useful productive concerns.'[27]

A major source for the origins of an urban middle class had been the bureaucracy. Late nineteenth-century Malabar witnessed a massive expansion of local government. There was the gradual substitution of custom by law and the growth of a highly centralized administrative apparatus which took over such duties that had been traditionally performed by village communities or large landholders. This provided a vast stratum with employment as government officials, from clerks to Deputy Magistrates.

During the colonial period, even though with the end of Company's rule, covenanted posts were technically made available to Indians, it was very uncommon to find Indians in responsible posts, as the British preserved their prerogative in keeping the most important posts for themselves. But, with the intention of making the administration cheaper, the colonial authorities ran the administration virtually through uncovenanted posts. Malabar was no different, with a number of Indians gaining entry as tax officials and other government servants.

The nineteenth century also witnessed the emergence of several new professions in Malabar as a consequence of colonial policies and institutions. One among them was the legal profession. During the British period, several law courts came up in different parts of the country. This was never meant as a benefit for the Indian people. As Rothermund writes: 'Spreading British justice in India was by the way no exercise in expensive altruism but, on the contrary, a good source of additional revenue. Stamp fees and court fees provided an income which far exceeded the cost of the maintenance of the judicial establishment.'[28]

The British system of justice had recognized individual rights, especially in matters pertaining to land property. When land became a saleable commodity, land litigation became common in Malabar.

A contemporary record states that 'with regard to litigation on land, in the last twenty years, Malabar contributed one-eighth of the Presidency, exclusive of Madras'.[29] Registration was inaugurated in this region in 1799, when a proclamation was issued stating that 'all writings in evidence of the transfer of landed property shall be registered either in the provincial or local adalats'.[30] This process got strengthened in the years to come. As the Gazeteer of the district points out, 'the effect of the Malabar Wills Act [of 1898] which placed the testamentary disposition of self-acquired property by persons subject to *Marumakkathayam* law on a secure basis, is beginning to make itself felt, the number of wills registered in 1901-02 being more than double those registered three years before'.[31]

Courts had begun to settle disputes traditionally done by the caste panchayats. By 1931, in Calicut district alone, there were 30 superior civil courts, far more than in any other district of the presidency. As Emree remarks, 'a society that places a high valuation on the rights of personal ownership of property will, of necessity, require a system of law and of courts to safeguard it'.[32] The literature of the times including Chandu Menon's unfinished novel *Sarada* and many of the short stories of Murkoth Kumaran are replete with references to lawyers and court life. The advocates, most of them Nairs and 'migrant' Brahmins, became symbols of power and soon constituted the most important segment of the middle classes, engaging in literary and public life.

Pleaders became a vital part of this new mileu. A provision was made for the parties to represent the suits through their agents or deputies if they were unable to attend in person. With this, an agent could plead for the party as *vakil*. In some cases, these *vakils* destroyed the already declining *tarawads*. In his memoirs, Moyarath Sankaran says of them: 'their job is to create new cases in the land. If anyone gets into their trap, they would ruin the person and the house. Most of them are unemployed Nairs who hate manual labour.'[33]

Professionals like doctors also came up during the early twentieth century. In 1854, the Government Headquarters Hospital had been set up in Calicut. In 1872, a mental hospital and in 1901, a hospital for children and women came into existence. The first medical school in Kerala was the one started in Calicut in 1914, from where the famous A. Balakrishnan Nair passed out. Around the same time, V.A. Raman started the first private hospital, Asoka Hospital in Calicut.

In her study of the middle class in nineteenth-century Bengal, Tithi Bhattacharya argues that education, at a time when colonialism limited all other channels of social mobility, was one of the most significant elements that made up the world of the Hindu *bhadralok*.[34] Development in Malabar throw up parallels. During the colonial period, like elsewhere in India, education had become democratized in Malabar. The missionaries and, later, the government provided the lower castes and females opportunities for acquiring education which, while being a major criterion for being a member of the middle class during the colonial period, now became a non-denominational space that was potentially open to all.[35] As caste and, to some extent, wealth gradually lost their earlier significance, Western education and government service acquired a newfound relevance in determining social status.

In the field of education, Malabar, during the colonial period, had always been one of the more advanced of districts. For most of the colonial period, though Malabar accounted for less than 8 per cent of the presidency's population, it had 10 per cent of the schools. In 1872-3, there were 34 primary schools with a total number of 1975 students.[36] In the early twentieth century, with the formation of the District Board, there was further advancement in the field of education. By 1936, the Malabar District Board ran twelve hundred schools, more than any other district in the presidency. These were complemented by philanthropists, who also started schools, the Ganapathy schools in Calicut being prime examples. By 1940, there were 2,81,259 male students and 1,92,475 girl students in public elementary schools.[37] In Malabar, there was not that much gap between male and female education. In 1951, male literacy was only about 1.6 per cent more than female. The tradition of matriliny among certain castes may have helped in diluting opposition to women's education. As Robin Jeffrey remarks, 'Kerala's culture gave women a remarkable independence, and women have made Kerala remarkably literate'.[38] In the field of higher education, four colleges that came up in the second half of the nineteenth century were to play a crucial role in the emergence of a middle class in

Malabar society – Brennen College in Tellicherry, Victoria College in Palghat, and Malabar Christian College as well as Zamorin's College in the city of Calicut, though for higher education, from the late nineteenth century onwards, well-off families sent their wards to Madras with the aim of training them for the government service or the legal profession.

The entire mechanism of the pre-colonial education order was challenged by colonialism. Nowhere was this felt more than in the new curriculum of the colonial educational institutions. According to one who went through the grid of a traditional educational system, earlier, 'the geography, history and arithmetic in most people's education were confined to what they knew of the landowning families. Geography consisted in knowing which family owned land in which places; history consisted in repeating the stories of great men who used to live or were still living in the landowning Namputiri families; and accounting consisted of calculating the amount of paddy produced in their lands.'[39] Now, modern subjects including the sciences were introduced, radically transforming the world view of a new generation of Malayalis.

Alongside the schools and colleges, training institutes came up for teachers. Only those who had the necessary qualifications could now teach in government and government sponsored institutions. As the indigenous educational institutions declined in numbers and prestige, the *nattezhuthachhanmar* – traditional teachers – were mocked. Even writers like Vengayil Kunhiraman Nayanar, popularly known as Kesari, who was otherwise not enamoured of English, criticized them for their lack of knowledge as well as cruelty to students, and claimed that 'anyone who can't shine in any thing else becomes one'.[40]

In late nineteenth-century Malabar, the new middle class did not constitute a high percentage of the population. According to the 1871 census, in Calicut, the most important of the towns in the district, out of a population of 48,338, there were only eighty government servants and 188 learned professionals.[41] At the end of the nineteenth century, the number of graduates, undergraduates and matriculates in the district was about 1,000 and the number of officials drawing a salary of more than 10, 20 and 50 rupees a month was 1,063,

245 and 90 respectively.[42] Though a minority, the influence of the middle class was disproportionate to their numerical strength, a fact acknowledged by the Malabar Marriage Commission in the context of their demand for marriage legislation: 'Though the minority that desires legislation is small, it is a growing and an educated minority, and every year will add to its strength and influence. The educated few are the leaven which will leaven the whole lump, and . . . their good example will in two or three generations . . . lead the rest to adopt the same standard.'[43]

Compared to the working class who gets mobilized against an exploitative other, the middle-class consciousness could have been limited. But in the lifestyle they followed and values they upheld, and in their anxiety to remain distinct from other groups/classes in society, surely, one can discern elements of 'class consciousness'. Moreover, consciousness, need not exist only when a group is aware of its economic interests. If we recognize that a group sharing similar views regarding how society, politics, law and culture should be organized also possess it, then, the middle class of colonial Malabar, who set the agenda on many of these fronts clearly fit the bill. The power of the middle class emanated from their ability to be cultural entrepreneurs.

Caste Composition

The new middle class came from different sections[44] even though, as the Statistical Atlas of Malabar, 1906, notes 'Nayars supply the bulk of the learned professions such as vakils and schoolmasters and a large proportion of those engaged in scriptory work.'[45] According to K.N. Panikkar, the reluctance of the British authorities to appoint as revenue and judicial officials those men of wealth and respectability due to their role in rebellions, threw open opportunities for the Nairs of weaker economic status. Amassing wealth using their official status they raised their social prestige. Their children who went to the government run schools and colleges ended up being *munsiffs*, magistrates and judges while they themselves had begun as petty village officials. The son of Vengayil Kunhiraman Nayanar, M.A. Candeth became the Director of Public Instruction, the first Indian in that post. It was this class which had the economic independence, and who had imbibed new cultural values that were at the forefront of the agitation for marriage and other reforms at the turn of the century.[46]

The middle class/caste interface varied across India. In Bengal, the *bhadralok*, except for the rare cases, were composed wholly of the upper castes. In Malabar, on the other hand, there was a significant presence of the lower castes among the middle classes. And, as Dilip Menon has shown, for them, unlike the Bengali *bhadralok* in the writings of Partha Chatterjee, colonial modernity provided a welcome relief.[47]

The Thiyyas, in spite of their relatively low social status in the Hindu caste hierarchy, produced a high percentage of middle class professionals and bureaucrats during the colonial period. In the mid-nineteenth century, Uppot Kannan and Dewan Bahadur E.K. Krishnan, both belonging to the Thiyya community, became deputy collector and sub-judge respectively. The community had made tremendous advances during the colonial period, so much so that one scholar thought that the 'Izhava story represents the complementary modern Indian trajectory of the famous "decline of Nayar dominance"'.[48] Thiyya links with the British, especially their women as concubines and wives of white army men stationed in Canannore, from early nineteenth century, not only improved their economic standing, but as some bigoted observers put it, their complexion as well. F. Dunsterville noted that,

> some of the Tierns in North Malabar are almost as fair as Europeans and are very handsome, possibly owing to an admixture of European blood. Initially, during the Company rule, a sizeable section among them had become economically prosperous through trading links with the English, which, in the course of time, even led to loose conjugal ties with the colonizers, 'their caste rules not making so much objection to temporary alliances as other castes'.[49]

Moreover, as there was a superstratum of Thiyya pundits throughout the land, the Englishmen used them as *munshis* to learn Malayalam. Naturally, therefore, there were several Thiyyas occupying clerical jobs, positions in the police department, and even junior executive posts in the revenue sections. In Malabar, as one writer put it, 'their growth is proven by the fact that . . . practically all the Indian-born higher officers in the administration until the second quarter of the twentieth century came from the Thiya community.'[50] In the late nineteenth and early twentieth centuries, there were several success stories in Malabar amongst the Thiyya community, most through education. P. Sankunny, who got into the Indian Education Service and retired as Principal of Teachers Training College at Saida Petta would be a prime example. He had his education, initially, at BEMP High School, Tellicherry, and later at Madras Christian College. Before joining the IES, he held stints as professor at Malabar Christian College and principal at Palghat Victoria College. Traditionally, toddy-tapping was seen as the occupation of the Thiyyas, like their counterparts in the south of the state, the Ezhavas. But once their economic position improved, and, consequently, their social status, by the middle of the twentieth century, scholars belonging to that community like A. Aiyappan had begun to strenuously deny that toddy-tapping had ever been the caste's 'traditional occupation'.[51]

It was, thus, the lower strata of the upper castes (Nairs) and the upper strata of the lower castes (Thiyyas) who, by acquiring English education, and, consequently, obtaining government jobs, constituted the majority among the Hindu middle class. On the other hand, the Nambudiris, the erstwhile privileged group in society took time to adapt to the new circumstances. Of course, a radical intelligentsia did emerge from among the younger generation in the group in the context of the reform movement led by the *Yoga-kshema Sabha*. But, for a significant section amongst the community as well as a few elite Nair feudal chieftains, loss of political power did not put an end to their delusions of grandeur. Turning their back on English education, they tried to maintain the indulgent life of the past, still possible through the possession of extensive lands. There were exceptions, of course. In parts of Calicut including Tali and Chalappuram, there were a number of renowned advocates hailing from the Tamil Brahmin community, most notably Manjeri Sundarra Ayyar, Congress activist and leading figure in the Theosophical movement.

Sources

As far as sources are concerned, novels like *Indulekha* written by the upper caste O. Chandu Menon and *Saraswativijayam*, authored by the lower caste, Pootheri Kunhambu, apart from dealing with the concept of romantic love, present the debates surrounding traditions and modernity in all its complexities. Lesser known works like the satirical novel *Parangodi Parinayam*, by Ramankuty Menon which countered the values contained in *Indulekha*, as well as *Storm and Sunshine*, an English novel written in the early twentieth century by the scholar, T.K. Gopala Panikkar, among others, have been consulted. Short stories of Murkoth Kumaran and others display the attitude of the educated middle classes' towards the archaic institutions of *Marumakkathayam*, *Sambandham* and the *Tarawad* system, and are situated within an urban milieu consisting of government servants, lawyers and teachers.

Prescriptive literature or manuals are also useful for reconstructing the social history of the period. But they should be handled with care since they were, in most cases, instructive without always being practised. Depending on them at face value can give a fake picture instead of the reality unless corroborated by other sources.

The essays of people ranging from Vengayil Kunhiraman Nayanar in the early twentieth century to Sanjayan in the mid-1940s have been compiled and are available in book form. Magazines of a wide range from college magazines of the period to *Mithavadi* brought out by the prominent Thiyya, C. Krishnan, *Unni Nambuthiri*, the organ of the Nambuthiri reformist group, *Gurunathan* and *Gurukulam* brought out by those engaged in the teaching profession to *Mathrubhumi*, under whose umbrella the differences of various sects and groups get subsumed under the over-arching ideology of middle-class nationalism are available. So too, some issues of the English *Malabar Quarterly Review* available in the libraries of Madras and Trivandrum. Native Newspaper Reports available in the Tamil Nadu State Archives contain extracts from some of the earliest newspapers in the region.

The autobiographical writings of some prominent members of the middle class who will appear in the coming pages are available.

They include those of K.P. Kesava Menon and C.H. Kunhappa, both involved with the publication of *Mathrubhumi*, and Balamaniamma, one of the earliest female literary figures from these parts. Then, there are the biographies of people like O. Chandu Menon, Murkoth Kumaran, C. Krishnan and Sanjayan. Like other memoirs and biographies of those from the subcontinent, they mainly deal with their public lives, and hardly touch upon their innermost emotions. Diaries, to some extent, help in overcoming this problem by revealing somewhat more intimate aspects of their life. They include the diaries of M.A. Candeth, K.P.S. Menon and G. Sankaran Nair kept at NMML, New Delhi.

Apart from the above-mentioned literature produced by the middle classes, for factual details, archival sources, including Censuses and other Government Reports have been consulted. Even though the history of every region is unique, developments elsewhere in the country and the world during corresponding periods have been taken into account. The attempt has been to unravel, through the writings left behind by individuals belonging to the group, a social history of the middle class in colonial Malabar by touching upon different facets in their everyday lives rather than a chronological narration of its growth.

Chapterization

The first chapter explores the world that the middle class inhabited. The cities which grew into prominence at the turn of the last century became avenues for a cosmopolitan lifestyle. The introduction and expansion of railways eroded physical and emotional barriers regarding travel and mobility as did the relaxation of caste restrictions. In the course of time, friendships arose cutting across caste and even racial lines. The cities also became the centres of a vibrant public sphere, but caste and gender exclusions ensured it remained devoid of any semblance of democracy and equality.

In the early twentieth century, when matrilineal *tarawads* were breaking down and patrilineal nuclear households were slowly replacing them, an educated elite in Malabar re-invented the notion of 'home'. In valorizing 'home', they were influenced by the colonial conditions they were living in, and the Victorian debates on domesticity. Inspite of women being placed at the centre of the domestic universe on paper, in reality, the father, the head of the family, remained its central element as the ultimate power in the domestic sphere including decisions concerning education and marriage remained in his hands. The second chapter examines how the middle class conceptualized 'domesticity' and how far it reflected reality.

The third chapter deals with the changing forms of leisure in colonial Malabar. Whereas, earlier, entertainment had been, one way or the other, linked to religion, now, secular ways of spending leisure became possible. At a time when physical health was stressed, games like cricket became popular. Forms of entertainment that were carried over from the past like Mohiniyattam were sanitized before being adopted by the middle class. At home, meanwhile, a newly literate people took to reading with a passion, while radio disseminated information as well as entertainment.

The fourth chapter takes up the question of caste in relation to the middle class. In late colonial Malabar, at the new workplace and in the public arena, the earlier legitimacy enjoyed by caste got eroded. Privileges based on birth counted for less; instead, evaluating an individual based on his internal values got stressed. People began to give up their caste-markers which, in an earlier era, had helped people identify different castes and behave accordingly in a highly hierarchized society. The new middle class, a product of the socio-economic changes unleashed by the British, was at the forefront in bringing about these changes. However, as would be shown in the last part of the chapter, the vestiges of the past persisted in the minds of a few, and at a deeply personal level, caste continued to play a significant role.

The last chapter seeks to examine the ambivalent response of the middle class towards colonial modernity. The approach, as the class grew in maturity, was to filter and selectively imbibe from Western civilization what was best for native society, while remaining rooted in one's own tradition. Those who blindly imitated the West were ridiculed, and the few who rejected modernity *in toto* got themselves sidelined from the progress the state was to witness in the decades to follow.

NOTES

1. Arnie J. Mayer, 'The Lower Middle Class as Historical Problem', *Journal of Modern History*, 47, September 1975, p. 409.
2. A good example of a work on the political aspects of the region's history would be Dilip M. Menon, *Caste, Nationalism and Communism in South India: Malabar 1900-1948*, Cambridge University Press, Cambridge, 1994; while the religious/caste dimensions in modern Kerala is addressed, among others, by George Mathew in *Communal Road to a Secular Kerala*, Concept Publishing Company, Delhi, 1989.
3. Morris Ginsberg defines a class as groups of individual who, through common descent, similarity of occupation, wealth and education, have come to have a similar stock of ideas, feelings, attitudes and forms of behaviour and on these grounds, meet one another on equal terms, and regard themselves as belonging to one group in varying degrees of explicitness. Morris Ginsberg, 'Class Consciousness', in *Encyclopedia of the Social Sciences,* Macmillan, New York, 1957.
4. Eric Hobsbawm, 'The Example of the English Middle Class', in Jurgen Kocka and Allan Mitchell, ed. *Bourgeois Society in Nineteenth Century Europe,* Berg Publishers, Oxford, 1993, p. 133.
5. Ibid., p. 142.
6. Geoffrey Crossick and Heinz-Gerhard Haupt, *The Petite Bourgeoisie in Europe 1780-1914: Enterprise, Family and Independence*, Routledge, London, 1995.
7. Patrick Joyce, *Visions of the People: Industrial England and the Question of Class, 1840-1914,* Cambridge University Press, Cambridge, 1992, p. 11.
8. Dror Wahrman, *Imagining the Middle Class: The Political Representation of Class in Britain, c. 1780-1840,* Cambridge University Press, Cambridge, 1995.
9. David Cannadine, *Class in Britain*, Yale University Press, London, 1998, p. 18.
10. Catherine Hall, *White, Male and Middle Class: Explorations in Feminism and History*, Polity Press, Cambridge, 1992.
11. Surendranath Banerjea, *A Nation in the Making*, Oxford University Press, Bombay, 1963 (1st pub. 1925).

12. Michelguglielmo Torri, 'Westernised Middle Class, Intellectuals and Society in Late Colonial India', *Economic and Political Weekly*, vol. 25, Issue No. 4, 27 January 1990, PE-9.
13. B.N. Ganguli, 'Conceptualising the Indian Middle Class', in K.S. Krishnaswamy et al. eds., *Society and Change: Essays in Honour of Sachin Chaudhuri*, Oxford University Press, Bombay, 1977, p. 27.
14. Sumit Sarkar, *Writing Social History*, Oxford University Press, New Delhi, 1997, p. 285.
15. Rajat K. Ray, 'Political Change in British India' in *The Indian Economic and Social History Review*, Vol.XIV, 1977, pp. 493-518.
16. Sumanta Banerjee, *The Parlour and the Streets: Elite and Popular Culture in Nineteenth Century Calcutta,* Seagull Books, Calcutta, 1998 (1st pub. 1989), p. 54.
17. Sanjoy Joshi, *Fractured Modernity: Making of a Middle Class in Colonial North India*, Oxford University Press, New Delhi, 2001.
18. The East India Company had established a factory at Tellicherry in 1683 to secure the pepper and cardamom trade, and on several occasions between 1708 and 1761, the company had obtained from the chiefs of the Kolathiri family and other local chiefs not only grants of land in and near Tellicherry, but some important privileges such as right to collect customs, and administer justice within the lands so granted.
19. Census of India, 1941, vol. XIX.
20. K.V. Joseph, *Migration and Economic Development of Kerala*, Mittal Publications, Delhi, 1988, p. 50.
21. Y.P. Chibbar, *From Caste to Class: A Study of the Indian Middle Classes*, Associated Publishing House, New Delhi, 1968.
22. K.N. Ganesh, *Keralathinte Innalegal*, Department of Cultural Publications, Thiruvananthapuram, 1997, pp. 382-3.
23. K.P. Rajasekharan, 'Vyavasayika Nagarathinte Randu Nootandu', *City Directory-97*, Calicut Corporation, Calicut, 1997, p. 67.
24. Jayaprakash Raghaviah, *Basel Mission Industries in Malabar and South Canara, 1834-1914: A Study of Its Social and Economic Impact*, Gyan Publishing House, New Delhi, 1990, p. 22.
25. K.P. Rajasekharan, op. cit., pp. 67-8.
26. G. Arunima, *There Comes Papa: Colonialism and the Transformation of Matriliny in Kerala, Malabar c.1850-1940*, Orient Longman, New Delhi, 2003, p. 110.
27. Anonymous, 'Is Malabar Progressing', *The Zamorin's College Magazine*, vol. I, no. 3, November 1912, p. 15.

28. Dietmar Rothermund, *Indian Economy under British Rule and other Essays,* Manohar, New Delhi, 1983, p. 5.
29. C.A.Innes, *Malabar,* Government Press, Madras, 1951 (1st pub.1908), p. 384.
30. Ibid., p. 385.
31. Ibid., p. 384.
32. Ainslee T. Embree, 'Land Holding in India and British Institutions' in Robert E. Frykenberg, ed., *Land Control and Social Structure in Indian History,* Manohar, New Delhi, 1979, p. 37.
33. Moyarath Sankaran, *Ente Jivita Katha,* P.K. Brothers, Kozhikode, 1965, p. 26.
34. Tithi Bhattacharya, *The Sentinels of Culture: Class, Education and the Colonial Intellectual in Bengal (1848-85),* Oxford University Press, Delhi, 2005, p. 2.
35. The colonial system of education, however, did not create an egalitarian society. Based on the theory that division of labour was the key to England's economic prosperity, the Wood's dispatch of 1854 had proposed, through education, to achieve a comparable system of stratification in India. Education for the masses was limited to 'useful and practical knowledge' in non-descript lower schools where funds were scarce while scholarships took a selected few to elite universities. This, according to Gauri Vishwanathan, produced a stratified society in which boundaries between the select few educated in English and the masses had grown so strong as to thwart the percolation of European ideas down to the latter in any form, even through translation. Gauri Vishwanathan, *Masks of Conquest: Literary Study and British Rule in India,* Faber and Faber, London, 1990, p. 151.
36. Report on Public Instruction in the Madras Presidency for 1872-73, no. XXXVIII, p. 63.
37. Report on Public Instruction in the Madras Presidency for 1939-40, vol. II, pts. I and II, pp. 35, 51.
38. Robin Jeffrey, 'Governments and Culture: How Women made Kerala Literate', *Pacific Affairs,* vol. 60, no. 3, Fall 1987, p. 471.
39. K.V. Moosathu, *Atmakatha,* National Book Stall, Kottayam, 1966, p. 7.
40. Vengayil Kunhiraman Nayanar, 'Nattezhuthachanmar', in *Kesari Nayanarude Krithikal,* The Mathrubhumi Printing and Publishing Company Ltd., Calicut, 1987 (1st published in *Vidyavinodini* in 1893), pp. 62-73.
41. *Statement of Population of 1871 in Each Village of the Malabar District Arranged According to Area, Caste and Occupation,* Govt. Gazette Press, Madras, 1874, p. 7.

42. *MMCR,* The Presidents Memorandum, p. 9 cited in K.N. Panikkar, 'Land Control, Ideology and Reform: A Study of the Changes in Family Organization and Marriage System in Kerala', *The Indian Historical Review*, 4, no. 1 (1977). In contrast to the West, in India, the middle class was also marked by their linkages to land. As K.N. Panikkar shows, those who secured government jobs or practised as advocates, also held Kanom tenure or belonged to 'tarawads' which had Kanom rights over land. Ibid., p. 38.
43. *Report of the Malabar Marriage Commission*, Lawrence Asylum Press, Madras, 1891, p. 43.
44 Even among the Mappilas, for long stereo-typed as backward, there were the occasional professionals and bureaucrats. Lord Pentland, Governor of Madras, on a visit to Malabar in 1913, in his reply to Himayat-ul-Sabha, notes that 'you now have a Mappila tahsildar, and a deputy superintendent of police besides a number of Mappila officers in the Registration, Police and Educational services with many representatives in the clerical posts.' *First Tour of H.E. The Right Hon. Lord Pentland, Governor of Madras (Coimbatore and Malabar)*, Govt. Press, Madras, 1913, p. 103.
45. *Statistical Atlas of Malabar*, 1906, p. 10.
46. Panikkar, op. cit., pp. 38-9.
47. Dilip M. Menon, 'A Place Elsewhere: Lower-Caste Malayalam Novels of the Nineteenth Century', in Stuart Blackburn and Vasudha Dalmia ed., *India's Literary History*, Orient Longman, Delhi, 2004, pp. 500-1.
48. Caroline Osella and Filippo Osella, 'Once Upon a Time in the West? Narrating Modernity in Kerala South India', in K.N. Ganesh, ed., *Culture and Modernity : Historical Explorations*, University of Calicut, Calicut, 2004, p. 45.
49. F. Dunsterville, *Illustrated Guide to the Madras Railway,* Higginbotham and Co., Madras, 1898, p. 52.
50. Cyriac K. Pullapilly, 'The Ezhavas of Kerala and their Historic Struggle for Acceptance in the Hindu Society', *Journal of Asian and African Studies*, XI, 1-2.
51. Osella and Osella, op. cit., p. 42.

CHAPTER 1

The World of the Middle Class

By the turn of the twentieth century, new towns were emerging while the older ones expanded further in Malabar. So did transport, especially railways, which was to have a huge impact on the lives of the people in the region. As caste restrictions lost their earlier potency and people became more mobile with the advancement in transport, barriers, both spatially as well as at the level of the individual, began to fade. Friendships arose between members belonging to different castes and even races.[1] Meanwhile, a public sphere along with a vibrant print culture developed in which the middle class would come into its own.

The Cities

By the late nineteenth century, Malabar had its share of towns, though, compared to the metros, they were small ones. In fact, as late as the 1930s, it was observed that, in Malabar, 'there are, to all intents and purposes, no real towns. Such few towns as there are being merely collections of bazaars or trading stations; and even these towns consist very largely of isolated houses in more or less extensive grounds of their own.'[2] Traditionally, Kerala did not have big cities. This is partly explained by the absence of a strong central political power structure and technological development. Urban forms did develop during the colonial period through a well developed transport network, but due to the absence of a central node which link all towns and contributes to a major share of urban population and urban economic activity, no big cities emerged. As a result, decentralized small towns became the feature of the Kerala landscape with little difference between urban and rural cultural pattern. The emerging social forms have been characterized as 'rurban' or semi-urban.[3]

Of the small towns then that existed in Malabar, the significant ones were Tellicherry and Calicut. The former, now Thalassery, is 21 km south from the present district headquarters, Kannur [formerly, Canannore]. It was established in 1663 by the British for the pepper and cardamom trade and was their first settlement on the Malabar coast, buttressed by a fort built in 1708. With the end of Mysore rule, and later the defeat and death of Pazzashi, Tellicherry rose into prominence possessing, among other things, the earliest light house in the state, port facilities, and a bridge on to the sea. It soon became a British centre with courts and government offices. Under the circumstances, the town soon acquired a cosmopolitan character with Arab, Gujarati, European, and Konkan traders selling their wares. C.H. Kunhappa, who studied in the BEMP School started by the Basel Mission with the help of the Parsees, refers to a 'Satram' near it, where every year 'the Chinese used to come with birds, coloured paper fans, etc., and in their amusing way eat with their small sticks'.[4] Writing in the late nineteenth century, F. Dunsterville found Tellicherry to be a 'healthy and pretty town built upon a group of well-wooded hills running down to the sea and protected by a natural rocky breakwater with suburbs 5 sq. miles ... trade consisting largely of the export of coffee, cardamoms and other spices.'[5] But Calicut, the former capital of the Zamorins later became the British headquarters in the district and the prinicipal town with a population in 1891 of 66,000, and a density of 4,000 per sq. mile.[6]

In the intellectual history of Tellicherry in the colonial period, names of a few natives stand out, O. Chandu Menon, in particular, who with his novel, *Indulekha* inaugurated a new era in Malayalam literature. Chandu Menon used a Malayalam, shorn of its Sanskritic trappings, and which was used by the common people, a trend that continued in the years to come through the works of authors like Sanjayan who too hailed from Tellicherry. As did Murkoth Kumaran, one of the earliest and most prominent short story writers in Malayalam. Then, there were a couple of foreigners who too contributed to the cultural well-being of the town – Hermann

Gundert and Edward Brennen. It was sometime in early 1839 that Gundert, a native of Stuttgart in Germany set sail on a ship heading to the south western coast of India. After several weeks at sea, he reached Tellicherry, and there, at his house given to him by the judge, T.L. Strange, on the slopes of a small hill overlooking the Arabian Sea, he spent the next twenty years with his French wife and children, engaging himself in missionary work. An indirect result of Gundert's work was the impetus he gave to the development of the Malayalam language. In 1847, he started the first Malayalam magazine, *Rajyasamacharam*, and a few years later, prepared the first lexicon in the Malayalam language. An elder contemporary of Gundert was the Englishman Edward Brennen, who after being shipwrecked on the coast of Tellicherry, spent years as an official at the town's port, and on retirement, before sailing back to England, left behind a small fortune for the native population to build a school which later developed into a college and survives to this day in his name.

Apart from the enormous cultural clout Tellicherry possessed during this time, the town also had considerable economic significance. Consequent to the development of Tellicherry as an important centre of English trade, a few native families, notably the Keyis, allying with the foreigners, made considerable wealth. Kozhikode would later on become the capital of the Malabar district, but all along, the cultural impact of the English rule would be most felt in Tellicherry reflected in the earliest cricket Association of the state, and the numerous bakeries which sprang up during the colonial period. Tellicherry had the most and best bakeries – Mambally bakery set up in 1880 being the earliest, and for long, at least until Independence, the most popular. The legend has it that an Englishman once, on Christmas eve, came to Mambally Bappu and ordered a Christmas cake. The cake was a hit, and the bakery never had to look back with long queues consisting of white women outside it a common occurrence in the years to follow.

One city to which a lot of Malayalis from Malabar were closely tied to during the colonial period was Madras. Ashis Nandy speaks of 'the beckoning magic of the new colonial metropolis'.[7] Until the middle of the twentieth century, Madras had remained the capital of a vast presidency comprising most of south India, and attracting multitudes of educated migrants from the distant parts of the region. Malayalis were no exception to this trend. In 1921, there were an estimated 8,000 Malayalis in the city.[8] And, by 1931, the figures had crossed 18,000.[9] A majority of the Malayali migrants were from Malabar which was part of the presidency. One important reason for this migration had been the economic stagnation Malabar experienced during the colonial period. An equally significant factor had been the demise of the *Marumakkathayyam* system, and the resultant partition of *tarawad* lands. As Susan Lewandowski observes, 'as land changes hands, more people became candidates for the rural to urban migration'.[10]

Some like Sanjayan and C. Krishnan went to Madras for their higher education at institutions like Madras Christian College and Presidency College. Others like C. Sankaran Nair took up residence there while practising law. Still others like Kesava Menon went there for medical assistance for his ailing wife, after giving up a career in public life in Calicut. Some got very attached to the city, and when the time came to leave it, felt bad. P. Narayanan Nair, who made his mark as a journalist and then as a freedom fighter, for instance, wrote 'while leaving Madras, naturally I felt sad.... There were some permanent lodges where law students, and government employees stayed. I was staying in one such lodge. I had been active in the functioning of Malayalee Club and the Kerala Samaj founded by Dr. C.R. Krishna Pillai and others.'[11] Madras offered a lot of avenues for a vibrant public life. For instance, Muliyil Krishnan used to go once a week to the Cosmopolitan club to have coffee, while he was at Madras working at the Presidency college.[12]

Those who studied in Madras came back to Malabar, and joined the government service as teachers, pleaders, clerks and revenue officials. Those who stayed back maintained close ties with their home and family in Malabar. Apart from the annual visits during vacations, occasions like birth, death and marriage also brought them home. Sometimes, relatives from Malabar came and stayed with their successful kinsmen in Madras.[13]

Madras, in spite of its many attractions to the educated middle classes, like other big cities, invariably had its vices which find a mention in one of Vengayil Kunhiraman Nayanar's short stories, 'Madirasi Pithalattam' where one of the characters get cheated by an acquaintance after being lured into consuming a spurious drink.[14] In fact, in an interesting article, A.R. Venkatachalapathy examines how in the popular imagination Chennai was perceived as a city of fraudsters out to cheat the gullible.[15] Other cities too seemed to share its vices. S.K. Pottekkatt recounts how a fraudster who befriended him in Bombay cheated him of the little money he had while on his very first visit to the city in 1934.[16] The towns in Malabar too had their pitfalls. The *West Coast Spectator* of 11 March 1916 reported that in Calicut 'brothels are everywhere, while certain localities about town are infested with fallen women to such an extent that it is dangerous to pass through them after night fall'.[17] But, still, for many amongst the lower castes, as Dilip M. Menon points out, modernity represented in the city was a liberating force. 'If the village is the space of caste and inequality and marked by the static continuance of hierarchy', writes Menon, 'the city is the transformative space in which new individuals can be forged as subjects unmarked by subjection. . . . *Sukumari*, set entirely in the city of Canannore with its fort, army barracks, armoury and camp bazaar, celebrates commerce over the moribund spaces of agriculture . . . [and] clearly establishes the link between escape from slavery, travel and social mobility.'[18]

Cities and towns looked a lot different then. It is hard to imagine, living in the second decade of the twenty first century, what the nights would have been like a century earlier. Electricity, for instance, was introduced in Kozhikode only in the 1930s, and even after that, for many years, inside many homes and on the streets, lamps were lit with the aid of kerosene. There was also much less traffic than now. And, for another, public places were dirtier and smellier! Even as late as the 1970s, in the early mornings, in many parts of Malabar including towns, scavengers used to carry night soil from homes in their little trolleys before shifting it to lorries, creating in its wake, an awful stink which would last for quite a while long after the vehicles had left. Kaattumadam Narayanan mentions how this activity used to spoil his breakfast while staying at Lakshmi Vilas lodge in Tali not far from its famous temple during a visit to Calicut.[19] Drainage system, meanwhile, was primitive, and the mosquitos played havoc with the health and lives of the people, a point repeatedly raised by Sanjayan in his writings.[20] The authorities were not too keen on the upkeep of sanitation. As filth accumulated around the Tali temple pond, and people complained, the colonial administration made it clear that this was not a public domain as the Zamorin, ex-raja of Calicut did not allow entry to the lower castes.[21] A.M.V. Hesterlow, writing at the close of the nineteenth century, observed that there was a problem with hygiene and personal sanitation in Malabar as rubbish and waste accumulated in compounds, soil and water were polluted by faeces, and cases of hookworm, dysentery and diarrhoea were the highest in the Presidency.[22] Health and sanitation, however, did improve over time. Mayer, writing a couple of decades later thought that the people of Malabar were cleaner than their counterparts on the eastern coast because of abundant water supply which allowed them to take a bath at least once a day.[23] Digging a well in Kerala which can provide potable water, as Joan Mencher points out, is not the problem that it is in other parts of India.[24]

Cities became the centres in the region for a nascent public sphere, a realm in social life where public opinion could be formed and a mediating role played between civil society and political power/state. The public sphere was the space in which new forces contended with the old order for hegemony.[25] It included, among others, Debating societies which mushroomed in the early twentieth century, one example being the Sri Jnanodaya Yogam founded in 1906 by some professionals in Tellicherry. It discussed matters pertaining to education, religion, and social reforms. At Calicut, K.P. Kesava Menon along with friends, mostly lawyers, used to meet every Sunday and discuss a pre-determined topic, at different homes.[26] Later at Madras, Kesava Menon and colleagues started the 'Neo-Fabian society' with 12 members including, among others, barrister K. Sankaranarayanan, K.P. Padmanabha Pillai and B.P. Wadia. They used to meet on Friday evenings at one of the member's house to discuss topical issues. Consequently, they also brought out books like the one on Montagu-Chelmsford reforms.[27] The Calicut Town hall, which came into existence in 1891, was to become the venue for many memorable public events including one in 1917, when K.P. Kesava Menon famously walked out of a meeting held to help the British war efforts when the Collector, Evans, refused to allow him to speak in Malayalam.[28] In 1903 was inaugurated the Annie Hall. It was from here that in 1917 Manjeri Sundarayyar and C. Krishnan started a procession for the rights of the lower castes to use the Tali temple approach road. Apart from these public halls, there were a few other avenues where such public meetings could take place, for instance halls set up in their own premises by certain well-off individuals. In Calicut, Lakshmi Vilas, the house of C. Krishnan had a hall named after his father (Paran), which held frequent public meetings, and where the likes of Bipin Chandra Pal, C.F. Andrews, Sardar K.M. Panikkar, Kumaran Asan and Ulloor spoke.[29] By the second decade of the twentieth century, public lectures on varied topics had become quite common, and often attracted a sizeable gathering. G. Sankaran Nair, who later gained fame as an advocate and Congress leader, notes in his diary of a crowded evening at YWCA where 'C.F. Andrews in khadi spoke on the message of love.'[30]

This public sphere thus constitued, however, was far from being egalitarian and democratic. It was, in the true sense of the term, a 'bourgeois public sphere' because it was largely organized by the bourgeois and petit bourgeois elements who spoke and acted on behalf of the rest of the society. In most cases, the criteria for admission into it were education and property ownership. And, as J. Devika has shown us, it also actively promoted gendering both in its very structuring and in the circulation of new ideals of gendered subjectivity.[31] In the dominant male discourse of the period, even as men occupied the public space, women were confined to the home. The few 'Sthree Samajams' that came up during this time did not question the gendered roles men and women had to play in the middle-class view of the ideal society. Even those *Sthree Samajams* that conformed to a dominant patriarchal view were showered with ridicule. The very need for such associations was discounted as men were expected to take care and protect their womenfolk whose nature it was to be dependent. It was pointed out that 'not only among human beings, but even among animals, "I" for a man constitutes his wife and offsprings. Their main objective is to look after their welfare.' If one continued to think along partisan lines, it was feared that 'soon we shall have *Bala Samajams* for children and *Purusha Samajams* for protecting men's rights.'[32]

Transport

Transport facilities improved during the colonial period. But, like everything else, the growth was painfully slow. Even well into the twentieth century, horse drawn and bullock carts were the mainstay on the roads of Malabar until they were replaced by hand drawn carts. Some bicycles, a few cars owned mostly by doctors, and a handful of buses constituted the other means of transport. That was all that was required in fact since people hardly travelled beyond their immediate towns and villages. P.K.S. Kutty, the cartoonist, remembers that during his childhood at Ottapalam,

> bus services were in their infancy. Small buses, which would carry about twenty people, used to run on twenty or twenty five mile routes. Carts drawn by bullocks or buffalos were the usual vehicle to go places. Some horse drawn carts too were there. Rickshaws, pulled by men, a common vehicle for locomotion, were used for short distances. A few chaps had their own cycles. The palanquin or the *manchal,* which four men carried from place to place, continued to be the carriers for affluent people. Ottapalam had a single taxi cab.[33]

Carts, which remained the chief medium of transport until the end of the nineteenth century, caused much havoc on the narrow roads.The *Kerala Sanchari* of 30 January 1889 invited the attention of local police 'to the annoyance caused to passengers in transit carts by the reckless and negligent way in which the carts are driven in Canannore, Tellicherry, etc. . . .' and went on to add that 'like in Presidency towns, no one should become a driver except when pronounced fit to do so by a competent authority'.[34] By the second decade of the twentieth century, however, motor transport had become common on the streets of Malabar towns. A fledgling motor transport system was not without its pitfalls. According to *The West Coast Spectator* of 26 September 1916,

The increasing popularity of motor traction in Malabar calls for the increased attention of the police and magisterial authorities. We are constantly receiving complaints of breakdowns and accidents which not only cause serious inconvenience, but result in injured limbs, and though not yet, lives. One does not, surely, like to be stranded in a strange locality in the dead of night by old engines and rickety cars. Stricter supervision by the authorities will be appreciated.[35]

The development in transport was closely linked to the promotion of the commercial interests of the English. Canals like the Conolly Canal built in 1871 helped reach commodities from the interior to the port towns on the western coast. In the 1930s, roads got concretized in Malabar. They connected the plantations on the high eastern land like Wynad with Tellicherry and Calicut. The Ponnani-Coimbatore road led to Tamil country. Then, there was a road at the heart of Malabar, from Palghat, through Calicut along the coast to Mangalore.

The railways came into existence here in the second half of the nineteenth century. The first tracks were laid between Madras and Beypore in 1861, which was extended to Calicut some years later in 1888. Over time, the railways got extended through Tellicherry, Canannore and finally up to Mangalore. More than other means of transport, railways best served British commercial interests. Goods from Malabar, including its timber could now reach Madras. The Nilambur railways was, similarly, meant to serve the interests of Nilambur teak plantation as well as the ones in Wynad, and those of the European coastal firms like Pierce Leslie & William Goodacre Co., Volkart Brothers, and Aspinwall & Co. who monopolized the export of plantation products as well as imports for the plantation sector. [36]

Meant initially to serve the British military and commercial interests, the railways hardly took care of the needs of the passengers. In the early years of its existence, traveling, especially in the third class compartments, was not a pleasurable experience. As *The West Coast Spectator* of 26 July 1913 commented 'third class traveling in India is certainly not a luxury. . . . Third class compartments on most railways are rickety, ill-ventilated, ill-roofed and ill-lighted.'[37] There were occasions during the rainy season when leaking carriages made it imperative for passengers to travel keeping their umbrellas open.[38] The racial discrimination the natives had to undergo while travelling was another handicap. The *West Coast Spectator* of 12 February 1916 reported that, 'While over-crowded compartments and cattle trucks are quite sufficient for the Indian passenger, Eurasians and Europeans, whether loafers or the lowest dregs of society . . . have comfortable compartments, specially reserved, and woe unto the Indian passenger who dares even to peep into the sacred enclosure.'[39] After mentioning how absence of level-crossings resulted in cattle being killed by moving trains, the *West Coast Spectator* of 15 April 1916 concluded that in this country, railway companies act on the principle that India is made for the railways, and not the railways for India.[40]

In spite of these limitations, the railways, like elsewhere in India, had a huge impact on Malabar society. It helped in bringing in goods, mail, as well as the latest fashion from among other places, the nearest metropolis, Madras. Its utility was widely acknowledged, and often led to strange demands. For instance, an article in the *Kerala Sanchari* of 3 July 1901 expressed the 'need for a railway station near Tiruvangad temple, as ladies around that area find it inconvenient to travel to the main station'.[41] The railways seems to have rendered unintended help to undesirable elements. The *Kerala Patrika* of 17 February 1917 draws attention to 'the facilities afforded by the present timing of the night trains to the thieves of distant places like Walluvanad and Palghat to go to Calicut, commit thefts there and return' and observes that 'a change in the timing of trains is highly desirable'.[42] It is said that the railways contributed to the people, even farmers, becoming conscious of the newly introduced clock time. In the school where P. Kunhanandan Nair (who later became more famous as Thikkodiyan)[43] was working, once, one of the union leaders, P.R. Nambiar came. It so happened that the office clock was not functioning. When asked how the school maintained its office timings, the reply was that by depending on the train timing – classes start at 10.15 a.m. when the local train passes towards north, and classes get dissolved in the evening when it moves south at 4.15 p.m.![44] The railway time would one day become the country's civil time as well, the Indian Standard Time, fixed five and a half hours ahead of the Greenwich Mean Time.

Railways soon became a part of the everyday lives of the people here. Different communities, in fact, tried to mould its growth according to their convenience. In the beginning, the Kozhikode railway station had an opening towards Pazhayangadi where Muslim rice merchants had their stores. When upper caste Hindus complained it was inconvenient for their womenfolk to walk through this street, it was relocated. Not all groups had their way, though. When the Thiyya community leaders requested the government to change the location of the station as one of their temples lay on its path, the government put down its foot and rejected their demand outright.[45]

New occupations, improvement in transport facilities, and the influence of modern scientific ideas helped break down several taboos, including those involving travel. Earlier, a Nair woman from North Malabar would not travel south of Korapuzha River, nor marry someone belonging to the same caste from across the river. But as a colonial official observed at the beginning of the twentieth century:

> to this rule there is what appears to be an exception, and this exception is now, having some effect, since of late years the world has come in touch with the Malayali who now-a-days goes to the university, studies medicine and law in the Presidency town or even in far off England . . . the old order changeth everywhere, and now-a-days Malayalis who are in the Government service and obliged to reside far away from Malabar, and a few who have taken up their abode in the Presidency town, have wrenched themselves free of the bonds of custom, and taken with them their wives who are of other clans than theirs.[46]

Moyarath Sankaran gives an instance of the breaking of the Kozhapuzha taboo in his memoirs, 'when Rairu Nambiar who practised a long time as an advocate in the Madras High court took his wife to Madras, the community was angered. But that patriot did not mind'.[47] Similarly, when K.P.S. Menon, from Ottapalam, married someone from Kottayam and practised law there, he nor his wife were ever forgiven for that. But by the next generation, these kinds of cross-regional marriages had become passé. Of Menon's two daughters-in-law, one was from Travancore, while the other came from Malabar.[48]

Anglo–Indian relations

Notwithstanding people having thousands of virtual friends on facebook and other such social media sites today, the size of the human brain, according to the anthropologist Robin Dunbar, does not allow for more than 150 meaningful friendships.[49] And, at the turn of the last century in Malabar, when caste restrictions were still in place, and under a colonial regime, the numbers must have been considerably lesser. In spite of an unfriendly atmosphere, however, friendships in their embryonic form cutting across caste and race did emerge.

In the backyard of St. John's Church, located between the Arabian Sea and a British-built fort in Tellicherry, lies the tomb of Edward Brennen, one of those Englishmen of the nineteenth century who, for the work he did for the land, remains much loved by the natives. His association with the town began on a stormy monsoon evening in the early 1850s, when following a shipwreck, he was washed ashore. For the next couple of decades, after that, he worked in different capacities at the port in the quaint little town. He made a lot of friends among the natives, and legend has it that in the evenings, after work, he would move around the town in his horse-drawn carriage, throwing, in the process, coins to the street children who would follow him.[50] After retirement, Brennen would go back to England, but before that, he would keep aside a big part of his savings for the establishment of an school for native children which functions to this day.

During the long period the English were in the country, they maintained close ties with certain families, especially those engaged in business. One fine example for this was the relationship they had with the Keyis of Tellicherry. The Keyis were a business family originally from Canannore, but in early nineteenth century, shifted their base to Tellicherry. Beginning with pepper trade, they soon delved into other businesses including timber. So rich did they become that sometimes the East India Company depended on them for loans. In return, the Keyis got unstinted support from the English authorities. So confident were the Keyis of this support that they would, with audacity, carry goods through the seas belonging to the Cochin raja without paying taxes. That this confidence was not misplaced became clear on more than one occasion including when the English establishment took the side of the Keyis in their dispute with the English planter, Murdoch Brown.[51] By the end of the nineteenth century, the equation had changed somewhat. Once they became the unchallenged power in this region, and the Keyis refused to upgrade themselves in their business activities, the English would have no time for them.

It was at Tellicherry that the British first set up their base, but later, Kozhikode was to develop into their headquarters. There, the English mostly stayed in the periphery of the town, at a height, in East and West Hills, very near to their barracks. But they continued to maintain friendships with the natives, one prominent example being Karunakara Menon. He started his career as a clerk in the English East India Company in 1801, but, before retiring in 1834, had gradually rose in the ranks. He played an important role in the English campaign against Pazhasi, so much so that one of the last requests made by the latter before succumbing to his injuries was that Menon should not approach him so as not to be polluted by someone who lived in close proximity with the English.[52] Menon was quite popular with the English officers, and when Captain Walsh visited Malabar, he spent a few days with Menon at his home in Ramanatukara, in the outskirts of Kozhikode, indulging in, among other things, hunting. Menon continued to be respected by the English authorities even after retirement, and was entrusted with the responsibility of mediating with the raja of Coorg against whom the English went to war in the early nineteenth century.

There were other examples too of what could be described as proto-friendships between the two communities. At the death of Churyayi Kanaran, who went on to become the Deputy Collector of Ponnani, Sir William Robinson, spoke thus: 'In this bereavement – so sore to you all – I too have lost the most esteemed and respected friend I have made in India- a friend of thirty years' standing and known to and respected by friends – especially our mutual departed one Mr Conolly long before that.'[53]

Chandu Menon, the novelist, enjoyed a good rapport with his English superiors which partly was responsible for his promotions, as well as the acquisition of the 'Rai Bahadur' title. He dedicated his second work *Sarada* to the Malabar acting District Collector, J.W.F. Dumergue, who had got his *Indulekha* translated into English, and thereby provided it a wider readership. Both he and E.K. Krishnan[54] were very close to Herbert Wigram, district Judge in South Malabar from 1875 to 1882, and, on the latter's departure from Calicut, arranged for the awarding of a gold ring each to whoever came first in Matriculation and F.A. at Kerala Vidyasala (later Zamorin's College) in his memory.[55] But this did not mean that Chandu Menon grovelled before the colonizers. One of his biographers cites an instance involving the hot-tempered Davids, the district judge, while Chandu Menon was a sub-judge. A Marar (a drummer) had gone to court complaining that the temple authorities had paid him less than what ordinarily a drummer would get during a festival. In order to decide on his talent, Chandu Menon asked him to bring along a drum and show his skills within the courtroom, which he duly did. Needless to say, those in the neighbouring rooms were acutely disturbed by what was going on. An angry Davids, after a peon sent to restore order failed in his mission, finally came to the spot himself. By then, Chandu Menon had judged that the Marar should be paid at the rate of an expert drummer. Though initially angry, Davids was finally forced to concede that Chandu Menon had been 'right in the matter, and shook hands with him'.[56] Others were even more forthright. One collector after taking office, as was the custom, met the editors of the local newspapers. On being introduced to Murkoth Kumaran, the editor of *Kerala Sanchari*, which had been critical of British officers, he said 'Mr Kumaran, my predecessor did not think much of you and your paper', to which Kumaran is said to have retorted 'nor did I think much of your predecessor'.[57] Some like the free-spirited Sanjayan quit his government job as a clerk at Calicut Hajoor office within months of joining as he had got tired of saluting higher officials.[58] In the biography of Madhavan Nair, there is a reference to how when he was a lawyer he once walked out of the court when the arrogant District Judge J.C. Stodartt scolded him for being late, and returned only after the latter apologized.[59] There must have been many other instances where Indians felt humiliated at the workplace – some responding in kind like Madhavan Nair did, others suffering in silence – for, as Sumit Sarkar says 'the office was also the point where the respectable, but struggling, Indian directly faced his predominantly foreign bosses, a situation marked by blatant distinctions in pay scales, racism, and insults which compounded the sense of the servitude of new jobs'.[60]

Print Culture

In the late nineteenth century, the world was changing in Malabar. Feudalism was giving way to a capitalist order. Individualism was beginning to make its belated appearance here. Caste was losing its earlier sheen, slavery ended, at least officially, and all had become equal before the law. Marriage was stabilized, and the nuclear family born. Horizontally and vertically, there was an expansion of education. Literacy rates were galloping at a tremendous pace, and there was, consequently, the creation of a reading public. Meanwhile, the Malayalam language was evolving into the one we see today, simple and of everyday parlance. Add to that the impact of the fiction being produced in the West. This was the context in which the Malayalam press, and ultimately the Malayalam novel emerged in Malabar. The introduction of the printing press, especially later in the vernacular, had a massive impact on society since it now ensured a far wider audience for the already existing local knowledge as well as the newly emerging ideas from the West. Print also helped sharpening the distinctions between neighbouring language communities, and thereby the development of modern Malayalam.

Print culture, which had its beginning in Malabar in the 1840s through the activities of the Basel Mission, proliferated at the turn of the century. In 1890, out of the ten printing presses in Kerala, three were located at Calicut. By the early twentieth century, apart from the publications run by religious and caste groups, there were also those brought out by the newly-formed professional associations like those of the teachers. No one liked to be left out, it seems. As the editorial of a college magazine, while justifying its existence, put it, 'Is there any profession that thinks it can go on without its magazine? Lawyers and barbers, carpenters and politicians, and last – of course not least – the Colleges!'[61]

The development of the press was closely linked to the evolution of Malayalam as a modern language in the nineteenth century. Ironically, it was a foreigner, Hermann Gundert, who, in many ways, contributed the most to this process. In 1851, Gundert brought out his book on Malayalam grammar, and in 1875, a dictionary in the language. In between, he also brought out a book on the region's history and geography titled *Malayalarajyam* in 1868. Missionaries like Gundert, no doubt, felt the need to communicate with the locals in the local language in order to spread Christian ideas. Not that there was no native contribution in the development of the vernacular. Malayalam had got its distinct identity from the days of Thunchaththu Ezhuthachan, the sixteenth-century devotional poet who, while discarding Sanskritic elements, had enriched the language with words from the everyday language of the common people, a legacy continued in the modern period by O. Chandu Menon, who in the preface to his first novel wrote 'this book has been written in the language ordinarily spoken in my home. . .'.[62] Later, Sanjayan, as his biographer observes, 'gave legitimacy to words discarded by the pundits, and as a result, ordinary people, unlike earlier times, began to read *Kerala Patrika,* edited by him'.[63]

The spread of government sponsored schools and colleges, which emphasized reading and writing skills, from the middle of the nineteenth century and the rise of a new educated middle class who took to reading literature also helped to gain universal acceptance for the Malayalam script. The expansion of trade and urbanization meant that there was the growing need for a literate section to deal with trade-related accounting. The content of Malayalam literature too was changing. The sacral was replaced by the secular. Mythology and scriptures were replaced by books on social sciences, natural sciences, technology, history, geography, and language. At the same time, prose took over from poetry as the dominant form of literature to articulate modern themes through fiction as well as non-fiction. Written prose became essential in government services, as the written orders in government circulars were usually in that form.

Malayalam had become the medium of self-expression for a conscious and articulate urban literati. This process got enhanced with the emergence of authorship in the language. According to Satchidanandan, 'literature' and the 'author' emerge as definite categories only with the formation of the public sphere in Kerala that was part of a general democratic movement of dissent, reform and awakening.[64] The primary requisite of a modern sense of authorship, the direct association of a piece of work in unaltered form with the person who produced it, was not a feature before the advent of print. But now, the author, with his individual style, was fixed to each word of his writing forever. The authorial institution was built up along with a new critical academy that came up with norms and standards gained especially from the Sanskrit and English classics that came to be widely translated into Malayalam.[65] On this process, K. Satchidanandan writes:

> The translations of Sanskrit and European classics provided new aesthetic norms and models. The codification of the rules of grammar helped the rise of a prose style; the pursuit of Sanskrit and western poetics led to the development of literary criticism. Fiction modeled after English, and prose narratives began to be written along with plays and verse narratives, epics, lyrics and other forms of poetry. Printing presses, newspapers, journals, publishing houses, libraries and literary societies promoted the growth of a secular and trans-class community of readers freely debating literary works.[66]

With a reading public now available, novels made their appearance. *Indulekha* was only one in a series of Malayalam novels which appeared in print at the turn of the century. Most of them enjoyed colossal success. This was, as Meenakshi Mukherjee points out, in spite of the central tension between realism and reality that existed in early Indian novels when the novelists imitated Western realism but the marriages of love they depicted was more or less absent here.[67] Dilip Menon says that some of the early Malayalam novels became a means of reform through other means. Given that a thoroughgoing reform anticipating modernity was inconceivable in Kerala under colonialism, given its hesitations on matters of custom, this project was, he says, taken up by novels written by late nineteenth- and early twentieth-century novelists belonging to the lower castes where the old caste self dies and the new, unmarked modern selves are located within the tropes of clean homes and secure families bound by love, a good example for this being Potheri Kunhambu's *Saraswati Vijayam* where a Pulaya convert to Christianity marries a Nambudiri woman after becoming a judge, which, in turn, becomes possible through the English education he has acquired.[68] However, this was not confined to lower caste novels. Pages of novels acting as public sphere long before meetings in town halls and debates in newspapers became a reality is also evident in the eighteenth chapter of *Indulekha,* where Madhavan, his father and uncle debate for long on various political and social issues at the home of their host in Bombay.[69]

Short stories were soon to follow. They would become even more popular as they dealt with everyday lives of ordinary people unlike the flamboyant novels, full of dramatic personalities, then being serialized in magazines. The translated works from the West had also become widely available by then. Those who professed to read and hoped to belong to the cultured elite stacked their shelves with books. Suri Nambudiri, the character representing the old order in *Indulekha* is bemused by the bookshelf he encountered in the sitting room of the heroine.[70] In *Sarada,* the hero Krishna Menon, instead of spending money on expensive clothes and ornaments, buys the latest books coming from the West, and in all, possesses around 2,000 books. All to good use, it would seem, as consequently, the government gives him a befitting job.[71]

Up to the end of the nineteenth century, at a general level, individualism and individuality were marked by their absence in the country. Instead one's destiny was more or less controlled by the institutions of family, caste, and community. The concept of self was to develop during the late colonial period. Autobiography, one of the forms in which the colonial middle class negotiated modernity, and documented transformations in society, was one of its expression. But every new genre of literature to thrive needs a receptive audience. So too autobiography. As Bhikhu Parekh suggests autobiography presupposes not only a unique self narrating itself but also a constituency interested in reading such narratives.[72] In Malabar, even as autobiographies proliferated, a sizeable section of readers interested in this form also developed.

Newspapers made their appearance even earlier. Gundert was a pioneer in this field. In 1847, he brought out *Rajya Samacharam*, the first newspaper in Malayalam from the press he set up in Tellicherry with the help of technicians from Mangalore. This was to propagate Christian values among the newly converted in order to prevent them from falling back to their earlier pagan culture.[73] Soon, he was also to start *Paschimodayam* to bring Western knowledge to these parts. Justifying its objective, its first editorial claimed that 'light does not emanate from the east alone. It comes from the west as well. Providence has ensured English rule over this country, and the resultant bridge connecting the two countries has allowed western knowledge to penetrate these parts. . .'.[74] The Missionary papers, though it contained no politics, included a rich variety of subjects in its pages including religious-moral education, literature, science, sports, and life history. Most of the early recipients were recent Christian converts. Dilp Menon believes, in Kerala, it was Christianity which provided the interface through which lower castes experienced modernity and allowed them entry into a public sphere. 'The missionary journals', according to him, 'democratized access to a literate sphere of debate and knowledge, and also provided an alternative sphere of reflection on self and society.'[75] The days of writing on leaves using nails were over. A new knowledge system made accessible through the machinery of printing to a hitherto deprived majority was emerging outside the ones controlled for long by the feudal-Brahmin groups.

A Malayali press with a purely Malayali perspective was to emerge much later, during the close of the nineteenth century. By then, an educated indigenous intelligentsia had emerged. At the turn of the century, there were three main newspapers in Malabar – *Kerala Patrika, Kerala Sanchari* and *Malabar Manorama*. Others were soon to follow, most of which had a reformist agenda. Vaghbatananda's *Athmavidyakahalam* attacked caste inequities and superstitions, while *Mithavadi* was an organ to espouse the cause of the Thiyyas. Defending its objective, in its very first editorial, it remarked that 'in Europe and America, groups, religionists and professionals bring out their own publications'.[76] Apart from other topics, it highlighted the careers of the successful amongst the community. Having a newspaper had become a prerequisite for any person or group that wished to become public, to press for their interests, and defend their opinions. Those who had acquired new education, mostly men, claimed authority and capacity to evaluate social life at the local level. This was to acquire perfection later in the satirical writings of Sanjayan who made it a habit to criticize the municipality on various issues including pollution, hygiene, corruption, etc.

By the time *Mathrubhumi* came into existence – as a newspaper in 1922, and weekly in 1932 – the Malayali press had come into its own. Though edited and owned by the predominantly Nair caste, by taking on caste inequities, reflected in its support for Vaikom *satyagraha* and espousal of the nationalist cause, it was soon to acquire the image and reputation of 'the national newspaper' from these parts.

Meanwhile, as print culture expanded, there were vociferous demands during this time for the setting up of reading rooms. One commentator, after arguing on the positive impact libraries had had in Western societies concluded that 'instead of wasting money to maintain loafers in temples, that amount should be used to set up libraries here.'[77] In 1924, there were twenty-eight registered reading rooms in Malabar with 2,802 members. By 1932, the number had risen to 50 libraries and 6,635 members. Among them was *Sanmargadarshini,* founded on 6 January 1929, with *Mathrubhumi* editor, P. Ramunni Menon presiding. A significant event in its early years was the visit of Gandhi, who was presented a copy of *Bhagavad Gita* and the token sum of 101 rupees.[78] Reading rooms had become such an important part of the new culture that in June 1937, a Malabar Vayanasala conference was held at Calicut to coordinate their activities. The public sphere had their enemies, though. The conservatives, still living in the hoary past, believed libraries would spoil the youth, destroy faiths, and pollute temples. Thikkodiyan refers to such opposition in his village when a Gramina Vayanasala was inaugurated by *Mathrubhumi's* founder editor P. Ravunni Menon. But the youth enthusiastically welcomed it as an opportunity for discussion and dramas.[79]

However, problems for a still infant press remained well into the twentieth century, not least being the financial worries. *Mathrubhumi*, inspite of its growing popularity, faced severe financial crunch throughout its early history, and, more than once, was on the verge of closing down.[80] Equally difficult was the inability to find contributors, a problem that led to the early demise of a few magazines. According to someone associated with the press, during this time,

> it was a period of transformation in Malayalam literature. Those who knew Sanskrit could not put it to use in Malayalam. Those who knew English had contempt for the Malayalam language and were reluctant to write letters, let alone, articles for the periodicals. Those who should have written did not write, and those who did write often did not know how to write at all, so that workers for periodicals like ours had to keep trying to encourage suitable people to contribute articles.[81]

While talking of the *bhadralok* in colonial Bengal, Sudipta Kaviraj points out that unlike in Europe, where there was a big gap between the origins of print culture and the emergence of a modern social group who could read and write, theirs was a case of being born into 'accidental modernity'.[82] This, it would seem, applies to the rest of India. Immaturity of a different kind, perhaps to be expected from a still nascent press, became evident in 1927, when *Mathrubhumi* got into trouble when somebody (as it turned out later, rightly) pointed out that one Savitri Antarjanam, who had been regularly writing articles and letters on behalf of reforms in the Nambudiri community did not exist, and what had been penned in her name had been the work of some reform-minded man from the community![83] But in spite of these difficulties, the potential of a vibrant press was seen by a few visionaries, not least Kandathil Varghese Mappila, who set up *Malayala Manorama*, Kerala's first Joint Stock Company. By the third decade of the twentieth century, a quite vibrant public sphere had emerged in Malabar, but it was a far cry from the egalitarian one envisaged by Jurgen Habermas. Women, at best, remained peripheral to it, their role mostly confined to home. That is the area we shall take up for discussion in the next chapter.

NOTES

1. Friendships going beyond castes are discussed in another chapter.
2. A.M.V. Hesterlow, 'Public Health of Malabar in Relation to Environment', *The Journal of the Madras Geographical Association*, vol. VI, October 1931-January 1932, nos. 3 & 4, p. 179.
3. T.T. Sreekumar, 'Urbanisation in Kerala, c. 1900-1981', MPhil. dissertation, CDS, Trivandrum, 1988, p. 65.
4. C.H. Kunhappa, *Smaranakal Matram*, Mathrubhumi Press, Kozhikode, 1981, p. 75.
5. F. Dunsterville, *Illustrated Guide to the Madras Railway*, Higginbotham and Co., Madras, 1898, p. 57.
6. Ibid., p. 42.
7. Ashis Nandy, *An Ambiguous Journey to the City: The Village and other Odd Ruins of the Self in the Indian Imagination*, Oxford University Press, New Delhi, 2007, p. vii.
8. *Census of India 1921: Madras XIII, Part II*, p. 95.
9. *Census of India, 1931: Madras, XIV, Part I*, p. 291.
10. Susan Lewandowski, *Migration and Ethnicity in Urban India: Kerala Migrants in the City of Madras 1870-1970*, Manohar, New Delhi, 1970, p. 95.
11. P. Narayanan Nair, *Ara Nootandilude*, Kerala Sahitya Akademi, Trichur, 1973, pp. 73-4.
12. K.M. Nair, *Muliyil Krishnan*, Norman Printing Bureau, Calicut, 1932, p. 83.
13. C. Sankaran Nair, for instance, brought his sister's son, C. Madhavan Nair to Madras, got him educated at Presidency College and then Law college. Once, he got himself established in the legal service, C. Madhavan Nair married his benefactor's daughter. Susan Lewandowski, op. cit., p. 108.
14. Kesari Vengayil Kunhiraman Nayanar 'Madirasi Pithalattam', in *Prabhandangalum, Kathakalum Mattum*, Bharatavilasam Press, 1956, pp. 178-84.
15. A.R. Venkatachalapthy, 'Street Smart in Chennai: The City in Popular Imagination', *In Those Days there was no Coffee: Writings in Cultural History*, Yoda Press, New Delhi, 2006, pp. 59-72.

16. S.K. Pottekkatt, 'Ente Bombay Jivitham', in *Ente Vazhiyambalangal*, Poorna Publications, Kozhikode, 2008, pp. 7-18.
17. *The West Coast Spectator*, 11 March 1916, NNPR for the Week ending 18 March 1916, p. 458.
18. Dilip M. Menon, 'A Place Elsewhere: Lower-Caste Malayalam Novels of the Nineteenth Century', in Stuart Blackburn and Vasudha Dalmia eds., *India's Literary History: Essays on the Nineteenth Century*, Permanent Black, Delhi, 2004, pp. 500-1.
19. Kaatumadam Narayanan, 'Kozhikodan Smaranakal', in P. Zakir Hussain, ed., *Kozhikode Orormappusthakam*, Olive Publications, Kozhikode, 2012, p. 102.
20. Sanjayan, *Sanjayante Theranhedutha Lekhanangal*, Poorna Publications, Kozhikode, 2006.
21. K.T. Seluraj, *Kozhikodinte Paithrukam*, Mathrubhumi Books, Kozhikode, p. 64.
22. A.M.V. Hesterlow, 'Public Health of Malabar in Relation to Environment', p. 182.
23. Adrian Mayer, *Land and Society in Malabar*, Oxford University Press, Bombay, 1952, p. 12.
24. Joan P. Mencher, 'Kerala and Madras: A Comparative Study of Ecology and Social Structure, *Ethnology*, vol. V, no. 1, January 1976, pp. 135-71.
25. Habermas defined the bourgeois public sphere as a realm where private people come together as a public for the purpose of engaging with the state, as a space of mediation between civil society and political power, where people relate to each other as equals. Jurgen Habermas, *The Structural Transformation of the Public Sphere: An Inquiry into a Category of Bourgeois Society* (tr. Thomas Burger), MIT Press, Cambridge, 1991.
26. K.P. Kesava Menon, *Kazhinja Kaalam*, The Mathrubhumi Printing and Publishing Company Limited, Calicut, 1986 (1st pub. 1957), p. 50.
27. Ibid., p. 64.
28. Ibid., p. 52.
29. Changarakumarath Sankaran, *C. Krishnan*, Sidhartha Book House, Trichur, 1967, pp. 33-4.
30. Diary of G. Sankaran Nair, dated 22 January 1922.
31. J. Devika, 'Negotiating Women's Social Space: Public Debates on Gender in Early Modern Kerala, India', *Inter-Asia Cultural Studies*, vol. 7, no. 1, 2006.
32. Kanippayyur Sankaran Nambuthiripad, 'Sthri Samajam', *Unni Nambuthiri*, vol. 7, no. 6, 1926, p. 356.

33. P.K.S. Kutty, *Years of Laughter: Reminiscences of a Cartoonist*, Thema, Kolkata, 2009, p. 10. Even as late as the 1960s, as Dr C.K. Ramachandran observes in his Memoirs, *Manchals* could be seen in Calicut and its surroundings either as the 'luxury cars' of the rich, or else, the 'ambulances' for the sick. C.K. Ramachandran, *Chikilsichum Chirichum,* Malayala Manorama, Kottayam, 2009, p. 15.
34. *Kerala Sanchari,* 30 January 1889, NNPR for the week ending 15 February 1889, p. 15.
35. *The West Coast Spectator,* 26 September 1916, NNPR for the week ending 30 September 1916, p. 1692.
36. C. Balan, 'Political Economy of Transport Infrastructure Development in Kerala during the Colonial Period', in C. Balan, ed., *Reflections on Malabar: Society, Institution and Culture,* The Post-Graduate Department of History, Nehru Arts and Science College, Kanhangad, 2000, pp. 35-9.
37. *The West Coast Spectator,* 26 July 1913, NNPR for the week ending 2 August 1913, p. 1201.
38. *Kerala Sanchari,* 18 July 1900, NNPR ending 31 July 1900, p. 105.
39. *The West Coast Spectator* 12 February 1916, NNPR ending 19 February 1916, p. 284. At the same time, the upper and middle classes were none too happy traveling with natives below their social rank. The desperate need they felt for physical segregation from those below them becomes evident in an article in *Kerala Sanchari* of 15 November 1889 which 'advocates the introduction of a fourth class on the Madras Railways in addition to the existing third class, the fare of which should be increased to a reasonable amount, but less than the second class fare, so that middle class people, who feel great inconvenience during their journey with the lower orders, may use the present third class.' *Kerala Sanchari,* 15 November 1889 in NNPR for the week ending 15 November 1889, p. 243.
40. *West Coast Spectator,* 15 April 1916, NNPR for the week ending 22 April 1916, p. 668.
41. *Kerala Sanchari,* 3 July 1901, NNPR for the week ending 6 July 1901, p. 268.
42. *Kerala Patrika,* 17 February 1917, NNPR for the week ending 17 February 1917, p. 457.
43. A fame gained from a career which spanned several years as a writer, theatre activist and AIR programmer.
44. Thikkodiyan, *Arangu Kanatha Nadan,* DC Books, Kottayam, 2008, pp. 127-8. K.S. Namboodiripadu, in his memoirs, writes of the trad-

itional method of calculating time before clocks and watches became popular – 'the most common methods of telling the time were *ativakyam* and *naksatravakyam*. Most people could tell the time by these methods as people can today by looking at a watch. The former depended on the position of one's shadow in the sun, while the latter calculated the time of night according to the position of stars, in particular, to the rising of certain stars....When it was overcast, and the sun and stars were not visible, certain instruments were made use of. They included a sort of sandglass made of coconut shell and a vessel with a small hole in it which, when placed in water, would gradually fill up and finally sink in the space of one *narika*, or twenty four minutes'. K.S. Namboodiripadu, *Ente Smaranakal*, vol. I, Panchangam Book House, Kunnamkulam, 1963, pp. 39-41.

45. K.T. Seluraj, *Innalekalile Kozhikode*, Mathrubhumi Books, Kozhikode, 2015, pp. 287-8.
46. F. Fawcett, *Nayars of Malabar*, Superintendent of Government Press, Madras, 1915, p. 7.
47. Moyarath Sankaran, *Ente Jivitha Katha*, P.K. Brothers, Calicut, 1965, p. 22.
48. Susan Lewandowski, op. cit., p. 111.
49. Robin Dunbar, *How Many Friends Does One Person Need?*, Faber & Faber, London, 2010.
50. A.P. Balakrishnan, 'Ennum orkkapedunna Europeanmaar', in *Thalasserry: Sarada Krishnayyar Memorial Fine Arts Society Smaranika,* Chitra DTP Solutions, Tellicherry, 2002, p. 22.
51. K.K.N. Kurup and E. Esmail, *Thalasseriyile Keyimar*, The State Institute of Languages, Thiruvanthapuram, 2009.
52. Prema Jayakumar, *Karunakaramenonum Eastindiacompaniyum*, Mathrubhumi Books, Kozhikode, 2009.
53. 'Churyayi Kanaran' Unsigned article in *Deepam*, vol. I, no. 8, Meenam, 1930, p. 3.
54. E.K. Krishnan, who was bestowed the title 'Dewan Bahadur' by the British government, ended his career as a sub-judge. His daughter, E.K. Janaki Ammal, obtained a doctorate from Michigan University, and served as a lecturer at Women's Christian College in Madras.
55. Murkoth Kumaran, *Oyarathu Chandu Menon*, Kerala Sahitya Akademi, Thrissur, 1996 (first published in 1932), p. 36.
56. P.K. Balakrishnan, *Chandu Menon: Oru Padanam*, Sahitya Pravarthaka Co-operative Society Ltd., Kottayam, 1957, pp. 32-4.

57. Murkoth Kunhappa, *Murkoth Kumaran*, Sahitya Pravarthaka Co-operatrive Society Ltd., Kottayam, 1975, p. 152.
58. Prabhakaran Pazhassi, *Sanjayan: Kalathinte Manasaakshi*, Department of Cultural Publications, Government of Kerala, Thiruvanthapuram, 2000, p. 48.
59. C.K. Moosathu, *K. Madhavan Nair*, Mathrubhumi, Kozhikode, 1987, pp. 43-4.
60. Sumit Sarkar, *Modern Times: India 1880s -1950s*, Permanent Black, New Delhi, 2015, p. 324.
61. 'Instead of an Introduction', *Malabar Christian College Magazine*, August 1932, p. 2.
62. O. Chandu Menon, *Indulekha*, DC Books, Kottayam, 2010 (1st pub. 1889), p. 21.
63. Pazhassi, op. cit., p. 63.
64. K. Satchidanandan, 'Everyday and the Avant-Garde: The Contexts of Modernism in Malayalam Literature', in M.A. Oommen, ed., *Rethinking Development: Kerala's Development Experience*, vol. I, Concept Publishing House, New Delhi, 1999, p. 25.
65. Ibid., p. 25.
66. K. Satchidanandan 'Renaissance, Decadence, Modernism and Post-modernism', Session 6, ICKS (International Congress on Kerala Studies)–A, vol. I, p. 70.
67. Meenakshi Mukherjee, *Realism and Reality: The Novel and Society in India*, Oxford University Press, New Delhi, 1985.
68. Dilip M. Menon, 'Caste and Modernity: Reading Saraswati Vijayam', *Studies in History*, 13, 2, n.s, 1997, p. 84.
69. O. Chandu Menon, *Indulekha*, pp. 218-61.
70. Ibid., p. 117.
71. O. Chandu Menon, *Sarada*, DC Books, Kottayam, 2008, (first published 1892).
72. Bhikhu Parekh, *Colonialism, Tradition and Reform: An Analysis of Gandhi's Political Discourse*, Sage, New Delhi, 1999, p. 280.
73. Though the editor's name is not given, it was probably edited by him. Price is not given which means that probably it was distributed free amongst the poor erstwhile lower castes.
74. Cited in G. Priyadarshan, *Malayala Pathrapravarthanam: Prarambha Swaroopam*, Kerala Sahitya Akademi, Trichur, 1982, p. 18.
75. Dilip M. Menon, 'A Place Elsewhere: Lower-Caste Malayalam Novels of the Nineteenth Century', in Stuart Blackburn and Vasudha Dalmia

eds., *India's Literary History: Essays on the Nineteenth Century*, Permanent Black, Delhi, 2004, p. 493.

76. Priyadarshan, op. cit., p. 127.
77. A.T. Devassey, 'Granthasalakal', *Gurukulam*, no. 8, July 1926, p. 20.
78. Anthony Pulikottil, ed., *Sanmargadarshini Vayanasala Platinum Jubilee Smaranika*, 2005, p. 35.
79. Thikkodiyan, op. cit., p. 38.
80. See Menon, op. cit., pp. 143-7.
81. K.V. Musathu, *Atmakatha*, National Book Stall, Kottayam, 1966, p. 78.
82. Sudipta Kaviraj, *The Unhappy Consciousness: Bankimchandra Chattopadhyay and the Formation of Nationalist Discourse in India*, Oxford University Press, New Delhi, 1993, p. 37.
83. P.C. Sukumaran Nair and P.M. Sudhakaran, eds., *Mathrubhumiyude Charitram*, Mathrubhumi, Calicut, 2000, pp. 140-1.

CHAPTER 2

Domesticity
In Theory and Practice

In a tract from Malabar of the early twentieth century, the 'home' was described as: '. . . one of the most sacred places on earth, where children possessing innocence akin to angels are born and grow up. This is the place made sacred through the performance of hospitality, and which provides fertile ground for the "divine radiance" of matrimonial love to emanate.'[1]

In the imagination of the middle class during the colonial period, as is clear from the passage above, 'home', counterpoised to the world outside, was given a great deal of importance.[2] By examining fiction and non-fiction produced in late colonial Malabar, this chapter tries to show how the new middle class conceptualized domesticity, and how far it reflected reality.

The House

Geographic features have exerted a striking influence on the distribution and pattern of settlement in Kerala. The physical features did not encourage compact settlements. The relatively high water table, coupled with the greater ease in boring through lateritic soil for wells, made dispersed settlements feasible. The ideal Malayali house generally built of laterite blocks set in mud or lime is, thus, set in its own compound with its food-producing trees including coconut, plantain, and jackfruit. According to one scholar, 'the form of the buildings with low walls, sloping roof and projecting canvas was mostly evolved from climatic considerations . . . for protection from excessive rain and intense solar radiation. The setting of the building in the open garden plot was again necessitated by the requirement of wind for giving comfort in the humid climate.'[3] Even as smaller houses inhabited by nuclear families were coming into existence, traditional large houses co-existed with them. It was in such a house at Vengalil near Calicut that V.K. Krishna Menon, who went on to become the Defence Minister of the country, was born and brought up at the turn of the twentieth century. Of the house, and other such types, his biographer says:

an old palatial house built with several courtyards in the '*naluketu*' style, one of the two styles of architecture prevalent then. In this type of house, rooms were clustered around a courtyard. Houses had four, eight, sixteen or more courtyards. Thus the size of the house could be determined by the number of courtyards. Vengalil was a 'sixteen *ketu*' and immense. The other style was called *padizhatapara*. This type of construction had a long outside verandah, with a parallel corridor inside. On this were two or three bedroom suites, with the reception and dining quarters at either end. In both these styles large quantities of wood, usually beautifully carved jackfruit, were used. The whole building was then capped with red tiles. The Kerala landscape, doted with these whitewashed red tiled houses was distinctive and picturesque.[4]

Of a house in the Malabar countryside, similarly, Dunsterville writes:

Outside the towns, the house of the better class of Malayalam Hindus are very prettily situated amid the rice-fields . . . narrow lanes divide the properties and the land upon which the houses are built is raised above the level of the fields, from which steps or ladders lead up to the house compounds. The gateways are very picturesque, with seats within on both sides, the doors are solid and quaintly carved: there is usually an upper room over the gateway with windows or openings through which in older times, retainers could fire at any approaching enemies. Between the gateway and the house the compound is full of big trees providing ample shade through the heat of the day; the main dwelling must face the east, and it usually has a wing on the two sides, north and south, the northern rooms being used for cooking and the southern for ordinary domestic purposes . . . upper stories are frequently added and wide, shady verandahs are to be found both up and downstairs: the woodwork of the dwelling-house is solid and substantial and often beautifully carved. . . .[5]

And, Mayer, while doing his research, stayed in a new Nair house in Chunangad, of which he writes:

> It faced east in a large compound of trees. Downstairs were bathroom, kitchen and a dining-room at each end of a broad veranda. Behind were rooms for stored paddy; above these were two bedrooms. There was no glass in the windows, which had shutters and were heavily barred . . . since the climate allows . . . most activities to be carried on in the open, . . . all Malayali houses have a veranda of varying size and elaborateness, and when it is uncomfortable or warm inside it is on the veranda that people take their food, receive their guests, and in the case of men, sleep.[6]

The above quotations suffice to give an idea of how houses of the well-to-do looked like in Malabar at the turn of the last century. Up to the beginning of the twentieth century, one's caste determined, like much else, the kind of house he or she lived in. Lower castes were not allowed to live in houses built with tiles, but as the influence of caste waned, gradually, these restrictions too gave way. Mayer,[7] for instance, observed that 'large houses are no longer the prerogative of the high castes, just as tiles, formerly forbidden to the lower castes can now be used by anyone who can afford them'. And, there was plenty of tiles to be had in the region with the beginning of a series of tile factories under the auspices of the Basel Mission. Wood too was much in demand, and, consequently, teak plantations were set up at different places, including famously at Nilambur by the district collector, Conolly. Meanwhile, domestic architecture too changed during the late colonial period. From the late nineteenth century onwards, alongside the traditional homesteads, houses constructed along modern lines, partly under European influence, were coming into existence in Malabar. The adaptations of European style to the climatic needs and the synthesis with traditional style are best seen in the bungalow architecture. The comfort requirement in the hot humid climate prompted the European settlers to go in for buildings with large rooms having high ceilings surrounded by verandah all around. Balconies for the upper rooms, porticos, and Venetian blinds which provided air circulation and privacy at the same time were some of the features of these new types of houses. Many houses belonging to the middle classes built during this period had, like the British bungalows, high roofs, verandahs, big windows, and porch for cars. Some Indians were living in bungalows similar to those used by the British. In fact, the house the sub judge lived in at Civil Station was bought from a Mappila, Mamukoya Haji, and, he did not have to do much innovation, after moving in! The homes of the Keyis, the business family from Tellicherry, similarly, with chandeliers, furniture made of mahogany, and porches were not unlike the homes the Europeans used to stay at that point in time. Keyis originally had their homes near to the sea where they lived in two-storeyed buildings, with the ground floor as their office, godown and shop, while the family lived upstairs. Later, they shifted their homes to the interior, with their godowns remaining along the coast.

In the fiction of the times, the ambience of these new homes is vividly described. In *Vasumati*, for instance, Murkoth Kumaran begins the story with the description of a bungalow belonging to a well-off Thiyya, one of the upwardly mobile lower castes, with a neatly kept garden outside, while inside, in the drawing room, the heroine plays harmonium, and the hero sits on a sofa amidst curtained windows, tables, and chairs.[8] In *Lakshmi Kesavam* written in 1892 by Padoo Menon, Devaraja Naidu's house has carpets, marble-topped tables, glass panelled cupboards, and oil paintings.

The ideal was the middle-class home in Victorian England. During his stay in England for higher education, M.A. Candeth, who later became one of the first Indian Director of Public Instruction, wrote thus of the house he stayed in:

> Very nice house, parallel walls, low ceilings, long nooks and fireplaces, the whole house ramblingly built. One of the country houses of which I have read so much. There is a very fine garden with hedges, small apple trees. Oh! All so lovely. . . . How nice English home life is . . . so lovely, so clean. There was a very nice gramophone. . . . At heart, I wish I were an Englishman. It is an honour to belong to this nation.[9]

A feature of Victorian middle-class domestic life had been the display of surplus wealth in over-cramped living rooms filled with curios. Home had become a site to express one's taste. Piano, sculpture, paintings, and a few green plants indicated a well- domesticated nature. In Chathu Nair's *Meenakshi*, the interior of the home is done up in the style of the Victorian bourgeois domestic spaces with painted mirrors, expensive carpets, sofas, chairs, glass lamps, and there is a library with two cupboards holding Sanskrit and English books.[10] Inside middle-class houses, in the sitting room, shelves lined with books had become the norm. In *Indulekha*, for instance, Surya Namboodiripad, who represents the old order, is stunned by the number of books kept on the shelves in the drawing room of the heroine.[11] At a time when, transport and communications were in their infancy, the home library was a window to the outside world. It encompassed the world within the confines of the home, and satisfied the desire to know the world without leaving home. In the photos available of public figures during this time, the background is almost always provided by bookshelves.

Some of the descriptions of inner spaces in novels and short stories might have been mere flights of fancy. But there are indications that, in some cases at least, they reflected reality. For instance, Balamaniamma, in her autobiographical writings notes the changes inside the home during her lifetime. During her childhood in the early part of the twentieth century, decorations at home were minimal, confined to shiny aluminium pots and tobacco boxes her grandma would place under the cots in dark small rooms. Later in her life, she was to live in modern houses where there were changes in architecture as well as decoration, which reflected both the changing role of women as well as her own individuality in nucleated families. There were gardens, high boundary walls and gates outside, while the interiors of the house would inevitably have a showcase with dolls, other toys, well bound books, kitchenware, and colourfully decorated handfans as well as Ravi Varma paintings on the wall.[12] Elsewhere, she talks of day dreaming or reading books on her red painted cot with the gods and goddesses painted by the very popular Ravi Varma looking down upon her from the walls.[13] Partha Mitter has written of how during the early twentieth century, reproductions of European paintings were replaced on the walls of Indian homes by the Indian mythological paintings of Ravi Varma, who, combining talent with professionalism and entrepreneurship, became the first Indian painter to break the monopoly of the European painters.

It should be borne in mind, however, that the description given above of the interiors of homes refers to those belonging to the very elite among the middle class. For the most part, in comparison to those of the present, the insides of middle-class homes then remained bare. As Mayer observed 'furniture is of the plainest in all houses. Other consumers' goods like razors, torches and bicycles are only starting to be popular among the middle classes in the country.'[14]

A section of the traditionalists did not take kindly to the mimicking of the West. Critiques of new forms of architecture in the pages of contemporary magazines are also a reflection of the changes taking place. For instance, it was pointed out that 'the blind imitation of western architecture in the construction of houses without properly comprehending it had resulted in the absence of beautiful houses, and the proliferation of fourth-rate English houses without taste. Like Varasiyar in *Parangodi Parinayam*, a drawing room was compulsory, even if the rest of the house is dirty – 'crowded with chairs and tables of little use or aesthetics; a gramophone in one corner, and a harmonium in the other just to look civilized'.[15] The range in the products the carpenter made is an indicator of the changes taking place in the interior of middle class homes. M.S.A. Rao, at the end of our period of study, wrote: 'a significant change in the articles prepared about thirty years ago can be observed. They [carpenters] were preparing mostly agricultural implements, cots, boxes, benches, doors and windows. Now they make chairs, tables, modern cots, almirahs, easy-chairs, tea-stools, dressing tables, mirror-stands. . . .'[16]

Another new development was the photograph, which, in the course of time, replaced portraits. While the aristocrats preferred paintings, the Middle class opted for photography partly because it was cheaper. Later photography would be privatized, even if expensive, but for a long time it was the studio people went to on important occasions in the family to record the moment for posterity. Most of the photos were taken from the studios which cropped up in different parts of the district, like Pinto studio in Tellicherry, Pithambhar and Nina studios in Calicut. Those who could afford, got theirs taken from home. As a form of inheritance these fixed images of the self and family – its changing lifestyles, family events – were stored for posterity on mantelpieces, and elaborate frames, or else, albums. Traditionally, in India, portraits and later photos of the dead ancestors were place alongside those of deities. So, photos, in a way, had been portends of death, but this did not prevent them from catching the imagination of the newly emergent middle class. As Malavika Karlekar points out, 'precious evidence of a recently acquired mobility and status, the photograph's value obviously outweighed likely proscriptions of caste and community'.[17] Several photos are available of the middle-class representatives in Malabar belonging to the first part of the twentieth century, the males in modern attire, in some cases where the photos had been taken at home, with shelves lined with books in the background, and later, photos of the whole family including women and children.

Middle-class homes, irrespective of the castes to which they belonged, laid a great emphasis on cleanliness. The anxiety to do so was more in the case of the lower castes, perhaps. Narayana Guru had exhorted members of Ezhava community and those below them to give importance to cleanliness, lack of which, he thought was one reason for their lowly status in society. The Christian missionaries too emphasized on this. Talking about the attempts by the central characters in the novel, *Sukumari*, to set up an ideal home space – where the floors are swept clean, cobwebs cleared from the roof, tables, chairs and stools are laid out, and the bed is made with a blanket covering it, Dilip Menon argues that 'the depiction of these "baubles of domesticity" and the insistence of cleanliness may have had much to do with a missionary rhetoric that related lower casteness to poor hygeiene. . . . Home as much as the clean family occupying a hygienic space was an absence that had to be imagined in detail before it could be realized.'[18]

Towards a Patrilineal Nuclear Family

Traditionally, among the Nambudiri Brahmins of Kerala, only the eldest son could marry. Younger sons were ideally expected to remain celibate and devote their lives to religion, but in actual practice, they formed permanent or semi-permanent liaisons, *sambandham*, with females belonging to the matrilineal caste – Nairs. The eldest son could also have these liaisons along with his legal marriages. According to Joan P. Mencher and Helen Goldberg, 'the liaisons were useful to the Namboodiris in two ways: (1) most obviously, to provide sexual partners for their younger sons, and (2), just as crucial to create useful connexions with important families.'[19]

Praveena Kodoth points out that legitimate cohabitation between men and women or fathering was not totally unknown in matrilineal Kerala, but these were rare, and, moreover, in the existing set-up, a property connection between father and children or husband and wife was not established. The principal property connection, thus, was between mother and children.[20] Kathleen Gough writes that among the Nairs, in the traditional system, marital ties, '. . . involved as economic obligations, only the husband's small seasonal gifts signifying continuance of the relationship, and other token gifts to establish legitimacy at the birth of a child. It did not involve co-residence, sexual exclusiveness, maintenance, or domestic services.'[21]

This combined with the fact that divorce was easy, flouted the requirements of a stringent colonial state with regard to marriage.[22] The British Indian civil courts, infact, had interpreted *sambandham* as constituting not marriage, but merely promiscuous intercourse. Apart from the colonial state, many educated Malayalis too were critical of the institutions of *Sambandham* and *Marumakkathayyam*. The objections are revealed in the following passage from the report prepared by the Malabar Marriage Commission:

> A Marriage law is an important aid to national progress and good morals. . . . *Marumakkathayam*, with the advance of education is becoming unworkable. It offends against every principle of political economy, and of healthy family life. It is based on the doctrine that there is no female virtue, and no sin in unchastity. . . . By freeing a man from the obligation of maintaining his wife and offspring, it sanctions the reckless propagation of the species.[23]

The colonial administration propagated the belief that a proper marriage system would improve the moral fibre of the matrilineal society, and rescue Malabar from a state of 'uncivilised barbarism'. Communal property, polygamous relationships, and matrilineal descent were seen as the vestiges of a savage, 'natural' past. It was hoped that private property and monogamous marriages with conjugal co-residence and patrilineal descent would herald the beginning of a civilized nation. In an anonymous article in *Kairali*, it was argued that 'one main reason for the hesitation of the Nairs to do any worthwhile work was the hitherto existing institution of joint family system which enabled anyone possessing property to survive on the wealth earned by somebody else in the past'.[24] Across India, during this time, the nuclear family was idealized in contemporary literature. Joint family system, for long in vogue, was losing its appeal. In his work on the making of the modern family in Bengal, Pradip Kumar Bose writes:

> Joint family was found to be inadequate because of denying individual identity, restriction of women in the household, heterogeneous influences on children, irrational imposition of authority, hierarchical arrangement of power and privileges sanctioned by customs but not validated by reason and lack of intimacy, informality and equality. . . . In contrast to hierarchy and authority, the new family was founded on sentiment and thus the sentiments of love, concern and affection within the family came to be celebrated and articulated.[25]

In Malabar, an emergent middle class, mostly Nairs, influenced by colonial propaganda and Christian moral notions regarding the permanence of marriage, began to demand changes in marriage laws and laws of inheritance. To articulate their views and expedite this process, the Malabar Marriage Association was founded in 1881. The Malabar Marriage Commission was set up in 1883, and out of those interviewed by it, a majority supported changes in marriage laws. Consequently, a series of Acts were passed which brought into reality monogamous marital unions, and, consequently, nuclear households. The Acts include The Malabar Marriage Act which sanctioned the registration of customary *sambandham* unions as legal marriage where the wife and children could claim maintenance from the husband (or father) without forfeiting their rights to property from the household. The Malabar Wills Act of 1898 gave right to individuals who opted for legal marriage to pass on their self-acquired property to their wives. In 1933, the Madras

Marumakkathayam Act was passed by the Legislative Council which effectively ended the *tarawad* system.[26] It legalized *sambandham* marriages, granted the right of adoption, and allowed branches the right to demand partition. It also legalized inheritance from father to son. Meanwhile, these changes as well as the various tenancy Acts in the twentieth century affected the Nambudiris which necessitated changes in their own community. The *Yogakshema* movement which was started in 1908 had, among other objectives, the reform of marriage laws within the community. Partly due to its efforts, the Nambudiri Act of 1933, was passed, according to which, younger Nambudiris could now marry Nambudiri girls, and *Illom* property could be inherited by the younger sons.

The break-up of the *tarawads* was a tramautic experience for many. In the case of the lower castes, however, since the great majority of families did not own any land, their changeover to elementary family units was relatively easier and many families among these castes gradually did so. The absence, or the limited amount of joint family property compelled individual members to take up occupations other than the family occupation, and this usually led to their forming elementary family units.[27] However, it should be noted that nuclear family hardly remained nuclear in many cases because when distant relatives, fellow villagers, and caste men, turned up for long stays, one was not supposed to turn them away.

Meanwhile, commercialization of agriculture, urbanization, trade and the service sector developed unabated as the century progressed. With the decline of *tarawads*, those who lost rights over land and revenue came to town in search of jobs. Nuclear families became the norm amongst them.[28] The old patriarchy was giving way to the new. The new patriarchy was, in some ways, a relief for the young brides – an escape from the clutches of their mother-in-law to a household where there existed the possibilities of an intimate and exclusive love relationship with a husband, and life as his educated and literate companion.[29] The father who, earlier in a matrilocal *tarawad* organization, was only a visitor and did not live with his children, now gained in prominence, and became the central figure in the family, officiating during important family functions including naming ceremonies. Earlier, children were under the legitimate guardianship of the *Karanavan*. At the turn of the twentieth century, the situation was changing. In a case, involving the custody of children, the Joint Magistrate of Malabar directed the restoration of children to the guardianship of their natural parents from that of their maternal uncle.[30] The father figure gets celebrated in the literature of the times, for instance, when in *Storm and Sunshine*, during a discussion on marriage, Raghava Kurup firmly states that '. . . a legal marriage and binding relationship of father and son is a test of civilisation.' In the *Wound of Spring*, Krishna Menon is more desirous of becoming a father with 'loving authority than enjoy the glory of a *Karanavan* with prestige and unquestioned authority'. By the 1940s, a large number of Nair students of Presidency College and Madras Christian College entered their father's name as guardians instead of their uncle's as in the past.[31] In short, a family now meant a network of individuals owning common properties possessing a name and a blood line, facilitating sanctioned sexual satisfaction and the reproduction of offsprings.

With fewer members, in the modern nuclear family, there was obviously less of the hierarchy and segregation in comparison to the old *tarawads* or joint families where homes were not homogeneous spaces. In a perfect Nambudiri *illam*, T.K. Anandi points out, there was spatial segregation between men and women, married and unmarried, and elders and youngsters. For Nambudiri women, the alignment of space within the *illams* indicated the nature of her work, her family position and also her ritual position connected with purity and pollution.[32]

The sanctity of marriage was upheld by contemporary writers. The freedom enjoyed by wives in a marriage was compared 'to a parrot, whose legs are tied to a long knot, being allowed to fly in the skies, or a deer being allowed to run around in a beautiful garden surrounded by high walls'.[33] At the same time, divorce which was becoming too frequent for comfort, was criticized – 'If a woman takes a liking for another man and decides to live with him after dropping her husband, we will end up becoming beasts. Marriage is a contract between two communities. Divorce is a violation of that. In no marriage is complete satisfaction guaranteed. If because of differences, we go for divorce we shall have time only for that!'[34] The importance attached to family and discipline within it becomes clear from the following passage in Kesava Menon's autobiography: 'Discipline is learnt from within the family. The atmosphere for the growth of love emanates from the family. The enthusiasm for doing public good also is generated from family life.'[35]

In traditional India, possibilities of romance in man-woman relationship were limited by institutions like child marriage, extended family households, and polygamy while elders within the extended family kept a strict watch on sexual morality. The influx of English romantic novels in the nineteenth century did bring about changes at least in the way man-woman relation was viewed. However, it remained more an ideal than lived experience for the most part. Pre-marriage courtship was an absolute rarity, and romantic love more likely happened post-marriage, especially in a nuclear family when colonial job requirements took the husband away from the joint family, and the wife accompanied him in his new place of work. Ideal marriages, then as now, were rare and while men, in such situations, sometimes took recourse to spending time with prostitutes or having an extra-marital relationship, women were left with no option than spend a life devoid of love with their faithless husbands. Sex was not thought of as a sin here until Victorian sense of morality was introduced.[36]

It was only in the late nineteenth century through the influx of English Romantic novels, influence of Victorian morality and the coming into being of nuclear families that romantic love emerged and got privileged over sexual love. In the literature of the times, couples exhibit their affection for each other in endearing terms. Love letters became an inevitable part of early twentieth-century novels. In *Storm and Sunshine,* Narain Menon writes to Madhavi:

My heart's love,

I should unchivalrously accuse you of a crime viz., that of stealing away my heart. My heart is with you. . . . My thoughts about you and my anxieties about the possibility of my cherished hopes being realized are ceaselessly eating out the vitals of my body. I wish you will reciprocate my feelings towards you. Even a favourable reply from you will be sufficient guarantee for my further existence in this world. My heart is full and words fail me. Reply.[37]

The reply was prompt:

Dearest lover,

In my turn, I should roll back upon you the charge you laid at my door. Instead of my stealing your heart, the reverse has been the case. I cannot write more just now but reserve everything for the evening when I hope to meet you at the tankside and I shall unbosom myself of all that I am full just now.[38]

Several arguments were made in contemporary literature to valorize love. For instance, it was argued that that 'love is not a temporary phenomenon, but instead is the infinite joy obtained when two souls meet and understand each other after a long separation. Love is the chain that binds man and the immortal soul, and is the basis for a complete life'.[39] Meanwhile the importance of sex was downplayed. One author pointed out that 'life without self control was akin to an unbridled horse-ride. . . . Both men and women should be conscious of the need for chastity.'[40] There were, thus, as J. Devika points out, calls for a disciplining of bodily desire, reserving it for the culmination of the love-relationship in marriage.[41] There must have been the odd marriage made in heaven, so to speak, with the couple spending the rest of their lives together in love. But, there were others where the ideal of love took a back seat, and were guided, instead, by more practical considerations. Before getting married, a young Sankaran Nair, for instance, mused thus: 'Many indeed are the miseries that human responsibilities, especially so, matrimony, bring in their train. I am resolved to marry if at all a rich girl. At least, I could then be rid of anxieties on that account.'[42]

Tanika Sarkar has argued that according to the colonial middle-class' world view, the Hindu male had allowed himself to be colonized and had surrendered his autonomy before the assaults of Western power knowledge whereas the Hindu women's unique steadfastness to the husband in the face of gross double standards, and her unconditional, uncompromising monogamy were signs that marked the Hindus off from the rest of the world and gave them an identity.[43] Though Malabar was not known for monogamous conjugal relations among many communities until recent times, here too, female chastity became a recurrent theme in the dominant discourse of the times. In a discussion on chastity, after taking the cudgel against the wayward sexual life of the Western woman, a woman writer wrote in *Mathrubhumi* 'chastity is when a woman obediently performs her wifely duties faithfully and sincerely to a man she has accepted as her husband out of her own volition and God as witness, accepting his bad qualities along with his good'.[44]

But, for some at least, the new-found passion for chastity was meant for the males as well. M.A. Candeth, while in London, was aghast at one of his friends' ways: 'I wish Menon and others would not walk about with girls in London. They spoil our name, our status. They forget that we represent our country here. People who are gentlemen at home rarely do these things.'[45] In the literature of the times, it was stressed that if matrimony was to become a success, faith and love should be its integral part, and if one of them gets damaged, the marriage was bound to get destroyed. The importance of monogamous love was stressed. 'Love for wife is the backbone of matrimony', opined a writer, 'if one enters another woman even in thoughts, he is more bestial than a wild animal'.[46] Sex for the sake of it was looked down upon. It was posited that 'in the mind of those who enter into marriage, two emotions dominate – sex and siring a child. The first one is beastly and temporary, while the latter is permanent and heavenly'.[47] Consequently, physical beauty, at least in theory, was not considered very important. While choosing a partner, it was warned that 'one should not just go for external factors, but instead look for a harmonious combination of both external and internal factors'. In the novel, *Storm and Sunshine* the author describes the love between the heroine and the hero 'Physical beauty, they did not admire. It was the mental beauty that implanted in them such a deep-rooted love. The man who loves a girl for her exquisite personal charm, or a girl who falls in love with a man for the same reason, generally repents afterwards because that love is not real, not lasting.'[48] In an extreme case where sex was downplayed and sexual abstinence emphasized, it was pointed out that 'a male should marry only after the age of 25-30 . . . after marriage, husband and wife should sleep in two separate rooms in the nights, and engage in different work . . . when lust becomes unbearable, one should pour cold water over one's head. . . .'[49] Middle-class pioneered social reforms, meanwhile, aimed, among other things, to eliminate customs like *Tirandukuli* (ceremonial bath after first menstruation) which could be seen as celebration of female sexuality.

The New Woman

As I write this in late 2016, at the Botanical Survey of India in Kolkata, a year-long exhibition on the life and works of E.K. Janaki Ammal, one of the pioneering botanists of the country is coming to a close. The many recognitions she received in her illustrious career include a flower being named after her, and the Padmashri, one of the foremost awards granted by the Government of India. And this, for a woman born in the late nineteenth century in a Thiyya family is a remarkable achievement.

In some ways, in spite of her caste and gender, Janaki Ammal had a privileged upbringing. Her father, E.K. Krishnan was a sub-judge at Tellicherry, and a profound scholar, who had close contacts with the important intellectuals of his time, plus a rich library at home. So the initial inspiration and skills came from home which she was to later on hone at the colleges and universities of Madras and the US.[50] She would come back to India from the US and spend the rest of her working life in teaching, doing research, for which she was, as we saw already, amply recognized.

So, Janaki Ammal's life took a different trajectory from what was usual in pre-independent Malabar. She remained unmarried all along, but was a great success in her professional life. But, as we will see in the following pages, lives of other women in colonial Malabar hardly resembled hers.

In Partha Chatterjee's opinion, as an alien rule established its sway over the Indians in the external domain by virtue of its superior material culture, the Indian intelligentsia gave shape to an inner space that was taken to be inviolate and autonomous.[51] The Hindu home was thus counterposed to the world outside which lay beyond their immediate power and control. With the strategic placement of the home, the Indian intelligentsia invented the new cult of domesticity, where women were to play a crucial role. According to the middle-class world view, women were in charge of the 'home', where men had to enter slightly bowed. There was a proliferation of manuals providing guidelines to women on managing the household. Home and women were to be protected from the conflicts and corruption of the outside world, where the menfolk often faced defeats in the material world. She was to be the spiritual and moral influence on the man. Home was to be the woman's sphere where she was to look after household management, control servants and children. In the middle class division of the world into public and private spheres, women's role was confined to the latter. The dominant view was that they should not have to go out and work for their maintenance, which should be the responsibility of the menfolk. The rationale for this was:

> There is and should be a division of labour. In every family there are two kinds of work – earning wealth and household work. Only men can do the former as that work entails staying far away from home for long hours. Due to problems like menstruation, pregnancy, child birth, child rearing, etc women cannot do that. Instead, they should concentrate on running the household.[52]

At a time when women's education had made advances, and the concept of companionate marriage had got entrenched in middle-class minds, it was widely agreed that women should not be tied up like cattle inside their homes. There were calls to improve the conditions in which women worked at home. 'For working in the kitchens, a writer declared, let us introduce some machines.'[53] The decline in the status of women, it was reminded, would destroy not only a family, or even a community, but the whole nation.[54] The 'ideal' type of woman portrayed in literature was someone who was educated enough to be a friend to the enlightened middle-class husband, in conformity with the concept of 'companionate marriage' popularized by Victorian sensibilities, but who would, at the same time, stay at home and perform her role as wife and mother to perfection. As Judith Walsh observes, 'love, literacy, the education of wives and the range of daily and domestic practices compatible with the demands of life in British-ruled India – all were mutually constitutive, mutually implicated in the lives young Indian men imagined for themselves. In their homes, they wanted system, order, efficiency, and hygiene; in their wives, literacy, education, companionate marriage and love.'[55] It was, for instance, pointed out by a college-going student in a college magazine that 'an educated woman is the boon companion of man, his guiding star.... If woman is to become a companion to man, if she is to have a place in society, then she must be well educated.'[56] 'An educated woman', the author went on to add, 'is essentially one with a moral backbone, a clear-sighted observer, serious in purpose, and never enticed by subtle ideas and fickle fancies'.[57] Thus based on a combination of Western morality, and imaginary notions of Indian womanhood, stereotypes of the New Woman were constructed.

As noted above, the education of women was expected to help 'create' this New Woman. From the late nineteenth century onwards, girls were being admitted to schools, but not always in institutions meant exclusively for them.[58] This invited criticism, and the *Kerala Sanchari* of 21 August 1889 drew the attention of the Directorate of Public Instruction to evils arising from sending girls to boys' schools.[59] But by the fourth decade of the twentieth century, attitudes had changed. It was, for instance felt that 'apart from the fact that co-education reduces expenditure, boys would not feel unnecessarily shy in the company of girls, nor misbehave with them if given a chance from a young age to mingle with them.'[60] More persistent was the disquiet regarding the content of education. It was felt that 'it was not right to have the same kind of education for man and woman as their duties are different . . . women should be taught child-rearing, *grihabaranam*. . . . The knowledge of the capital of Madagascar would not help in that.'[61] In an article informed by current patriarchal values, the editor of a women's magazine wrote of the need to restructure women's education in which 'housekeeping' was to get pride of place in the syllabus, and which would include courses in primary economics, cooking, child-rearing, etc.[62] It was feared that in the present educational system, where they do not get adequate opportunities for rest nor exercise, women would have lost their health and beauty by the time they completed their education, and would not be able to live up to their roles as housewives and mothers.[63] In the novel *Indulekha*, whereas Madhavan's education is geared to gain him employment and thereby independent income, the heroine's is of a private nature meant mainly to sanitize the mind. In Malabar, by the 1940s, the percentage of girl students to female population was 10.6 which was the second highest in the Presidency.[64] However, a dominant male discourse ensured that very few girls went for higher education, and even those who did, ultimately ended up staying at home, performing household chores.[65] Even someone like K.P. Kesava Menon, educated at Madras, editor of *Mathrubhumi*, and a congress leader of prominence by the 1920s, writes in his memoirs that even though his wife was educated only upto the fourth standard, it did not matter as she was adept in household matters, and that to someone like him who was particular about food, her culinary talents came as a blessing.[66] Similarly, G. Sankaran Nair makes the same point in his diary when he says this about his wife – 'poor Ammu has to do the whole work at home. And I am happy to note that she does it most willingly, gladly and ungrudgingly. I am really fortunate in not having for my wife a specimen of the so-called modern woman'.[67] Muliyil Krishnan, lecturer at Presidency College in Madras, kept an English teacher to tutor his semi-educated wife, sixteen years younger to him. Everyday, before going to college in Madras, he used to assign 'homework' to her in order to improve her handwriting and knowledge in maths. It is not clear whether her English and maths improved, but Krishnan's biographer points out that she became adept, like many other women of her generation and class, at cooking, once winning first prize in an 'Indian Food competition' organized by the National Indian Association.[68] The new conceptions of sexual difference built upon existing traditions ensured that women stayed at home, and the few who ventured out had to face the consequences. Revathy Amma, wife of a police commissioner at Mahe recounts in her memoirs how her attempts at a life outside the home even in philanthropic activities came in for much criticism.[69] Similarly, Parukutty Amma, a character in the *Wound of Spring*, after a stint as a music teacher, finds a life of isolation at home.[70] Under the circumstances, the sole objective in a woman's life was to find an ideal husband. It was pointed out that 'the biggest thing for a woman in material life is marital happiness, and to gain a conducive husband for that.'[71] While talking of her childhood in Malabar, the poet Kamala Das refers to one woman in her neighbourhood who ended up being a spinster because no one was willing to marry her as she was too highly educated![72] Some women did try to combine qualities of a good housewife with their own creative and commercial initiatives. For instance, Madhavi Amma, wife of C. Krishnan, though she spent her time mostly in the kitchen, had started her own business from home – 'Mrs Krishnan's Malabar Medical Store', specializing in Ayurvedic medicine, which soon attracted orders from even distant Ceylon, Burma, Singapore.[73]

This is not to say that resistance was not offered by women to the gendered roles prescribed by patriarchy. In several of the early writings by Malayali women, there are instances of an alternative vision regarding how society should be organized.[74] And, in the twentieth century, as J. Devika has shown us, there was the gradual expansion of women's spaces beyond the home, in 'non-coercive' institutions like schools and hospitals, where women's attributes of kindness and goodwill came in handy. This allowed women to move out of a certain limited domain without losing their claim to womanhood.[75] But until the end of the colonial period, such instances were few, and were more the exception than the rule.

Elsewhere, J. Devika has pointed out that 'among the classes engaging with modern ideas in late nineteenth and early twentieth century Kerala, gender came to be presented as the "natural" alternative to Jati-based social order, one that seemed to be based on something readily apparent and concrete, even unambiguous, i.e. sexual difference'.[76] Women were generally identified with their sexuality, their bodies, and men with their minds, their energy. The former became the figure of fragility who had to be protected from the outside world. Sexual differences were stressed and masculine and feminine characteristics constructed to buttress the distinctive roles men and women were to play. Men as citizens of the world outside had to be tough, rational and aggressive whereas women who were to live out their roles as dependents in the form of wives and mothers were to be patient, kind, and show restraint, apart from possessing beauty and aesthetic sensibilities. In one instance, where this line of argument took extreme proportions, it was posited that 'just as breasts look good and natural on women, so too music and poetry when they possess them. . . . Men's qualities are their masculine exploits. For women, it is beauty. . . . Sweetness resides only in their throats. Men with sweet voice cannot be men.'[77] Madhavi, the heroine in *Storm and Sunshine*, is shown studying Sanskrit and music, the latter for which 'her silvery voice and diligence and grasping intellect peculiarly suited her'.[78] The interests of men and women were also seen as being different. For instance, it was pointed out that,

> when a new sari is displayed in a shop, a woman would not leave without looking at it twice. They talk about dress while traveling in train, and while going to meetings. They go to marriage parties not to bless the couple, but to see what other women have come wearing and also what the new bride is wearing. . . . Where men meet, in clubs and elsewhere they argue about games, politics, Karl Marx, but never dress. . . .[79]

It was believed that man's masculinity depended on his ability to provide for his dependents. The feminity of his wife and daughters depended on their capacity to be dependent. A man's dignity lay in his occupation; a woman's gentility was destroyed if she had one. A husband who could not provide order at home was looked down upon. Some belonging to the middle class found it difficult to combine public life with their family life. Indulging in the former prevented a few from providing sustenance to their family. A good example would be K.P. Kesava Menon, who, with his wife increasingly becoming ill, had to give up his public life as well as the editorship of *Mathrubhumi* – which was anything but remunerative in those days – and go first to Madras, and then abroad. When, it appeared that his wife was expecting another child, G. Sankaran Nair noted in his diary 'I fear she is getting pregnant. God help her and me. My family seems to grow and it is high time that I took to my own affairs instead of spending all my time for the public.'[80] The reverse, was also true. For those men whose family life was a failure, there was the possibility of fulfilment in the world outside. K.P.S. Menon, who would later have a glittering diplomatic career, after revealing his share of problems at home, consoled himself thus: 'Felt perfectly miserable as Chima is becoming more and more indifferent. How the romance of our marriage has fled. I feel she does not care for me. The old spontaneity is gone. But it is all my own fault. Why should I, after all, allow myself to be wrapped up in a mere girl. I have other interests in life, enough to make man ignore such worries.'[81] For women, there was rarely such duality; home was their 'all in all', the 'natural' site of their feminity.

As Dipesh Chakravarty, among others, has shown, in the middle class debates of the period it was often argued that regeneration of the nation must begin at home. It was believed that tranquillity in the nation was not possible until serenity was established at home, and the nation cannot improve until the individual did. The internal discipline of the European home with its cleanliness, hygiene and punctuality was seen as the key to European prosperity and political power. The domestic was, thus, seen as an inseparable part of the national. The public sphere, it was felt, could not be erected without reconstructing the private.[82]

An ideal mother was expected to bring up her son so that he grows up into an ideal member of civil society, a responsible citizen expected to fulfil the needs of the nation. A manual for the mothers' during this period pointed out that 'the responsibility of mothers is more difficult as well as important than engineers constructing new buildings, a commander commanding an army in war, or even an emperor ruling over an empire. . . . Mistakes committed by them could be rectified, but not those made by the mothers.[83]

In the educational set-up of the period, as indicated earlier, girls were to be trained only as future mothers, not future citizens. The role of mothers in raising children was time and again emphasized. It was pointed out that 'there is no sound more valuable to an Indian than "mother". . . . Terms like "patni" indicate the sacred status women have in Indian matrimony.'[84] One article ended with the call, 'sisters, your duty is twice that of man. The two identities you have in the world are those of wifehood and motherhood. You are responsible for rearing boys who shall be future citizens, and girls who shall, in the future, become wives and mothers.'[85] Women who were expected not only to produce children, but also raise them, apart from looking after the husband and the household were 'to possess a modicum of knowledge in health science, psychology and economics'.[86] The present government was criticized for fixing the syllabus without taking into consideration gender differences.[87] It was opined that in the teen age, 'girls should be taught *Kilipatus* and *Puranas* apart from Health science, especially children's health, and cooking as the reading of such literature along with music provide the household peace and happiness'.[88] Those women who did not conform to the new ideal were ridiculed by the likes of the satirist Sanjayan.[89]

According to Dipesh Chakravarty, two kinds of women were termed 'Alakshmi' by the Indian middle class during the colonial period. One, those without formal education as it was they who brought the nation into disrepute. In *Premabandham,* in the very beginning, when wife Ammukutty playfully disturbs him when he was working, Kesava Menon scolds her and complains of her lack of education.[90] Second, those who through education, became arrogant, lazy, immodest, defiant of authority, and neglectful of domestic duties.[91] In contrast to the self-centred and self-seeking woman of the West guided by a materialist yearning, the stereotype of an all-sacrificing Indian woman steeped in spiritualism was constructed. In an article titled 'Oriental Woman', it was observed that 'an oriental woman leading a spiritual life and viewing the whole universe with compassion is not bothered about legislative assemblies nor franchise'.[92] It was pointed out that basically the orient and the occident were different. Thus, morality and ethics for the two were bound to be different. It was felt that there was no point trying to transplant one's values to the other without considering local specificities.[93] Those women who became highly Westernized, and forgot their roots were ridiculed. 'Instead of developing her own natural physical beauty,' it was observed, 'she runs after decoration in dress and ornamentation. And while dismissive of her own sweet voice, celebrates the ragas emanating with difficulty from the music machine. . . . If you tell her to water the jasmine plant in the garden, she will say she is too tired, and instead, knit well into the night in the dark and ill-ventilated interiors.'[94] Husbands of those women who did not conform to the expected norms were seen to require help and protection from their potentially dangerous wives. As one sarcastically put it,

> There are organized efforts on to protect the tenant from the oppression of the *jenmi*, the worker from the capitalist, the debtor from his rich creditor, and the nephew from his *karanavan*. But it is a pity that there is not any such equivalent attempt to save from the wife the husband who, in effect, is more oppressed than any of the ones mentioned.[95]

Changes in the Attire of Women

Reform movements of the twentieth century had highlighted the low position occupied by women in society which was seen as the sign of a civilization in decline. Of the Nambudiri women, who remained, like the rest of the womenfolk in the state, half-naked, it was observed that 'until and unless their status is low and they remain undecorated, Nambudiri community shall never attain glory. . . . Let us make these unfortunate women human beings by providing right education, decent clothes, and appropriate ornaments.'[96] Consequently, improving the position of women became a central part of the reformist agenda. This was to include, among other things, a change in their appearance as well. The ideal was represented by, among others, Ravi Varma, in whose paintings, the heroine is not only modestly covered in a sari but wears a blouse as well.[97]

Exposure to the outside world, made possible through modern means of transport, opened the eyes of a traditional society to its own drawbacks. As Mayer observed 'there has crept in lately, chiefly amongst those who have traveled, a feeling of shame in respect of this custom of dress (or lack of it!)'.[98] A dramatic change in traditional attire was the consequence. In the second decade of the twentieth century, it was observed that 'nowadays, all upper-caste women wear bodices, though bare-breasts are not considered immodest for Cherumas. Coloured saris are starting to displace the traditional white cloth. . . .'[99] The movement calling for changes in attire had to face opposition from the conservatives especially in the southern part of the state. Opposition to the sartorial changes, sometimes, came from within the family. For instance, C. Kesavan, in his Autobiography, writes of how when his mother wore a blouse, she was beaten up by her mother-in-law, after which she confined the wearing of blouse only in the presence of her husband in the bedroom.[100] In *Rithumati*, a drama written by M.P. Bhattathirippad, when the heroine, an English educated Brahmin girl wears a blouse for the first time, her old fashioned uncle/guardian tears it off in anger.[101]

In Malabar, under direct colonial rule, sartorial changes were smoother.[102] In clothing themselves, the Thiyya women, for instance, in the north of the state did not have to struggle like their lower-caste counterparts in the south. This was partly due to the effect of direct colonial rule in Malabar, and the proximity some Thiyya families enjoyed with the colonizers through marriage and otherwise. This could also be explained by the fact that the Thiyyas, though considered socially inferior, enjoyed numerical superiority and economic independence in many of these areas. Logan refers to Thiyya women from Canannore to Calicut covering their breasts with a cloth thrown over the left shoulder and brought forward under the right arm and tucked in behind or in front.[103] In the early twentieth century, as is revealed in novels like *Vasumati* written by Murkoth Kumaran, Thiyya women under Parsi influence, became pioneers in the wearing of sari.[104]

Childhood and Domestics

Malayali parents, in comparison to their counterparts in other parts of the country, were not very effusive in their show of affection as far as their kids are concerned. It was pointed out that 'in general it is not in the Nambudiri character to fondle and be indulgent towards children. If others are seen doing it, it is considered a piece of foolishness. When other people are present, Nambudiri women behave as though they speak to their own children only in order to scold them.'[105] The same could have been said for fathers, and parents in general in other communities as well during this period.

But things would change gradually. Earlier, during a period of domestic production, after infancy, a child became an adult, helping in the production process. Now, there was a long process through which a child went through before attaining adulthood.[106] Childhood attained importance during this time which is reflected in the fact that autobiographies inevitably devoted the first and often long chapter on this part of one's life. A child was now an object of love, providing a lot of joy to devoted parents. As someone put it, 'a child having the traits of both husband and wife, a source of great joy, was somebody to shower all your love on'.[107] Manuals appeared telling housewives how to raise children. In well-to-do families, separate physical spheres were kept aside for the children. To keep the kids amused, a variety of toys became available in shops specializing in them.

In the new nuclear households, keeping a domestic servant became a criterion of social distinction; every middle-class housewife wanted one. Attitude towards them was a bit ambiguous, though. The mother was to be entrusted with the rearing of the child. And where the mother would fail in her duties, with the servant taking up that role the manuals written during this period on the subject would castigate her in no small measure. Normative texts on child-rearing denounces servants for their bad influence and ill-treatment of the children. Murkoth Kumaran who authored a Mothers' Manual, cursed 'those lazy mothers who, out of consideration for their own convenience, beauty and health put the responsibility of feeding and bathing their children to paid Ayahs'.[108] The latter was also blamed for depriving the young mothers of any kind of physical exercise.[109] But, lived experiences were sometimes radically different from the contents of these normative texts.[110] Murkoth Kunhappa recollects how Koran, one of their servants, had his wedding at their house, and his son, who was born and brought up there, stayed with them even after his father's demise. Later he became a peon, and when Kunhappa's mother lay dying, sent a disconsolate letter accompanied by a five-rupee note.[111] While talking of Krishna Menon's childhood, his biographer mentions how the children were taken wherever they wanted to go by a horse-drawn carriage, the coachman of which was their cherished friend. When the latter got unfairly implicated in a criminal suit, Krishna, though still a child, volunteered to go to court as a witness for the hapless coachman who was finally acquitted.[112] In some cases, the domestics were an extended family. K.V. Moosath had a very close relationship with his ayah. He writes how 'like most children among Nambudiri Brahmins, until I was a few years old, I spent more time with my Nayar nursemaid than with my mother, and for that reason I was as fond of my nursemaid as of my mother. At night too, I slept next to my nursemaid, right up to my sacred thread ceremony at the age of nine.'[113]

In general, though the imagined 'home' in middle-class discourse remained more of an ideal, for, in reality, it remained a place seething with internal conflicts – male-female, master-servant, as well as family-individual. In spite of women being placed at the centre of the domestic universe on paper, in reality, the father, the head of the family, remained its central element. The ultimate power in the domestic sphere including decisions concerning education and marriage remained in his hands. But life was not devoid of fun altogether as new forms of leisure activities emerged both within and outside the home as the next section will try to show.

NOTES

1. Kundur Narayana Menon, 'Nammude Sthrikal Padikkendathu', *Lakshmibhai*, vol. 7, no. 12, 1912, p. 2.
2. Inspite of differences in specificities, following urbanization after which the division between 'home' and the 'world' gets pronounced, in middle-class discourse, there is a universal valorization of the former. For instance, the middle class of England in the nineteenth century, found 'the market place . . . dangerously amoral. The men who operated in that sphere [thought they] could save themselves only through constant contact with the moral world of the home, where women acted as carriers of the pure values that could counteract the destructive tendencies of the market.' Catherine Hall, 'The Sweet Delights of Home', in Michelle Perrot, ed., *A History of Private Life,* vol. IV: *From the Fires of Revolution to the Great War,* Harvard University Press, Cambridge, Massachusetts, 1990, p. 74. According to John Tosh, a home was seen by the English middle class as a haven from all the troubles in the outside world, to spend with your wife and children,

where there would not be intruders to destroy your peace and privacy. John Tosh, 'The New Men: The Bourgeois Cult of Home', in *History Today*, vol. 46 (12), December 1996, pp. 9-15.

3. Balagopal T.S. Prabhu, 'Kerala Architecture', in P.J. Cherian, ed., *Essays on the Cultural Formation of Kerala: Literature, Art, Architecture, Music, Theatre, Cinema*, KCHR, Trivandrum, 1999, p. 65.
4. Janaki Ram, *V.K. Krishna Menon: A Personal Memoir*, Oxford University Press, New Delhi, 1997, p. 1.
5. F. Dunsterville, *Illustrated Guide to the Madras Railway*, Higginbotham and Co., Madras, 1898, p. 53.
6. Adrian C. Mayer, *Land and Society in Malabar*, Oxford University Press, Bombay, 1952, p. 48.
7. Ibid., p. 48.
8. Murkoth Kumaran, *Vasumati*, Sriramavilasam Press, Kollam, 1935, p. 257.
9. Diary of M.A.Candeth, 20 September 1907.
10. Chathu Nair, *Meenakshi*, B.V. Book Depot, Thiruvanthapuram, 1949.
11. O. Chandu Menon, *Indulekha*, DC Books, Kottayam, 2010 (1st pub. 1889), p. 117.
12. Balamaniamma, *Ammayude Lokam*, Priya Publishers, Trichur, 1982, p. 10.
13. Balamaniamma, *Jeevithathilude*, Mathrubhumi Printing and Publishing Co. Ltd.,, Kozhikode, 1969, p. 120.
14. Adrain C. Mayer, op. cit., p. 124.
15. Patathil Padmanabha Menon, 'Adhunikarude Anashasyangalaya Chila Anukaranangal', *Kairali*, vol. 3, nos. 7-8, 1918, p. 270.
16. M.S.A. Rao, *Social Change in Malabar*, The Popular Book Depot, Bombay, 1957, pp. 41-2.
17. Malavika Karlekar, *Re-visioning the Past: Early Photography in Bengal, 1875-1915*, Oxford University Press, New Delhi, 2005, p. 72.
18. Dilip M. Menon, ''A Place Elsewhere: Lower-Caste Malayalam Novels of the Nineteenth Century', in Stuart Blackburn and Vasudha Dalmia eds., *India's Literary History: Essays on the Nineteenth Century*, Permanent Black, Delhi, 2004, p. 506.
19. Joan P. Mencher and Helen Goldberg, 'Kinship and Marriage Regulations among the Namboodiri Brahmans of Kerala', *Man*, 2:1 (n.s), March 1967, p. 89.
20. Praveena Kodoth, 'Shifting the Ground of Fatherhood: Matriliny, Men and Marriage in Early Twentieth Century Malabar', CDS Working Paper, May 2004, p. 7.

21. Kathleen E. Gough, 'Variations in Matrilineal Systems', in David Schneider and Kathleen E. Gough, eds., *Matrilineal Kinship*, University of California press, Berkeley, 1961, p. 595.
22. Kodoth, op. cit., p. 7.
23. *Report of the Malabar Marriage Commission with Enclosures and Appendices*, Lawrence Asylum Press, Madras, 1891, p. 36.
24. Innathe Nayanmar, 'Kshayichu varunna Oru Jati', unsigned article, *Kairali*, p. 23.
25. Pradip Kumar Bose, 'Reconstituting Private Life: The Making of the Modern Family in Bengal', in Ghanshyam Shah, ed., *Social Transformation in India*, vol. 2, Rawat Publications, New Delhi, 1997, p. 514.
26. G. Arunima believes that the *tarawad* that was attacked from the late nineteenth century had been a young creature - a product of the 'court-made law', which had adversely affected the tenants, cultivators and other dependents including the younger members of the *tarawads*. G. Arunima, 'Multiple Meanings: Changing Conceptions of Matrilineal Kinship in Nineteenth and Twentieth Century Malabar', *The Indian Economic and Social History Review*, 33, 3 (1996), p. 300.
27. T.C.Varghese, *Agrarian Change and Economic Consequences, land Tenures in Kerala, 1850-1960*, Allied Publishers, Calcutta, 1970, p. 98.
28. K.N. Ganesh, *Keralathinte Innalegal*, Department of Cultural Publications, Thiruvanthapuram, 1997, pp. 230-1.
29. Judith E. Walsh, *Domesticity in Colonial India: What Women Learned When Men Gave Them Advice*, Oxford University Press, New Delhi, 2004, p. 87.
30. B. Govindan Nambiar, *Handbook of Malabar Law and Usage as Administered by the Courts*, 1899, ALV Press, Madras, p. 9.
31. Susan Lewandowski, *Migration and Ethnicity in Urban India: Kerala Migrants in the City of Madras 1870-1970*, Manohar, New Delhi, 1970, p. 121.
32. T.K. Anandi, 'Home as the Sacred Space: The Household Rituals and the Namputiri Women of Kerala', in K.N. Ganesh, ed., *Culture and Modernity: Historical Explorations*, University of Calicut, Calicut, 2004, p. 147.
33. K.V., 'Vivaha Mochanam', *Unni Nambuthiri*, vol. 8, no. 12, Chingam, 1928, p. 496.
34. Ibid., p. 499.
35. K.P. Kesava Menon, *Kazhinja Kaalam*, The Mathrubhumi Printing and Publishing Company Limited, Calicut, 1986 (1st pub. 1957), p. 22.

In another work, K.P. Kesava Menon talks of how familial affection seemed to be missing in Western homes and how many Englishmen generally do not enquire about their parents or siblings for years together, and strictly settle even small monetary transactions with their own mother. When asked why this was so, he was told by an English friend that 'too much love for the family would come in the way of lording over such a vast empire!' K.P. Kesava Menon, *Bilathi Visesham* (1st pub. 1916), Mathrubhumi Books, Kozhikode, 2007, p. 115.

36. For a detailed analysis on the subject, see, Tapan Raychaudhuri, 'Love in a Colonial Climate: Marriage, Sex and Romance in Nineteenth Century Bengal', *Modern Asian Studies* (2000), 34: pp. 349-78; Rajat Kanta Ray, *Exploring Emotional History: Gender, Mentality and Literature in the Indian Awakening*, Oxford University Press, New Delhi, 2001 and G. Arunima, 'Friends and Lovers: Towards a Social History of Emotions in 19th and 20th Century Kerala', in Bharati Ray, ed., *Women of India: Colonial and Post-colonial Periods*, Sage Publications, London, 2005, pp. 139-58, have tried to show that India's own version of love existed in the pre-colonial past. B. Rajeevan, meanwhile, argues that Malayalis did not possess a sexualized subjectivity in the pre-colonial period. According to him, earlier, sex had the sole purpose of reproduction in a caste-based hierarchized society. A sexualized subjectivity emerged and the caste-based bodies got transformed into sex-bodies only later during the colonial period, with the gendering that took place in missionary-run schools. European notions of nudity led to the Shanars, among others, in the south to agitate successfully for the right to cover their breasts. Later, Sree Narayana Guru famously spoke of how human beings are of the same species, and that the only tangible difference is between men and women. Kumaran Asan's poem 'Duravastha', where the lower caste Pulaya consummates love with a Nambudiri woman, for Rajeevan, symbolizes the triumph of sex/love over caste divisions. B. Rajeevan , 'From Caste to Sex: A Study on Sexuality and the Formation of Modern Subject in Kerala', in *Rethinking Development: Kerala's Development Experience*, vol. I, Concept Publishing House, New Delhi, 1999, pp. 45-59.

37. T.K. Gopala Panikkar, *Storm and Sunshine: A Novel Illustrative of Malayalee Domestic Life*, The Norman Printing Bureau, Calicut, 1916, p. 67. During this time, though, romantic love remained more of an ideal, with love marriages hardly occurring, and an overwhelming majority of the marriages taking place within the same caste, where

individual preferences hardly mattered. Visible changes in this regard were to happen later in the second half of the twentieth century.

38. Ibid., p. 67.
39. N. Narayanan Elayathu, 'Pourasthya Vanithakal', *Mathrubhumi Weekly*, vol. 10, no. W22, 2 August 1932, p. 26.
40. Oru Bharatiya Vanitha, Charitriyavum Vyabhicaharavum, *Mathrubhumi Weekly*, vol. 11, no. W4, 10 April 1933, p. 8.
41. J. Devika, 'Negotiating Women's Social Space: Public Debates on Gender in Early Modern Kerala, India', *Inter-Asia Cultural Studies*, vol. 7, no. 1, 2006.
42. G. Sankaran Nair, Diary, dated 27-04-1922, NMML.
43. Tanika Sarkar, *Hindu Wife, Hindu Nation: Community, Religion and Cultural Nationalism*, Permanent Black, New Delhi, 2001, pp. 23-52.
44. Vanitha, op. cit., p. 9.
45. Diary of M.A. Candeth, dated 6 January 1909.
46. C.V.K.Elayathu, 'Dambathiyathil Sukhamundo Illayo', *Mangalodayam*, vol. 17, no. 10, September 1930, p. 715.
47. K.V., op. cit., p. 500.
48. T.K. Gopala Panikkar, op. cit., p. 92. This, maybe, was an ideal which many found difficult to emulate. In reality, beauty was much appreciated. Chandu Menon, who created a heroine of ravishing beauty in his first novel is said to have been repulsed by those with ugly looks, and used to wonder aloud why God created such imperfect beings. Murkoth Kumaran, *Oyarath Chandu Menon*, Kerala Sahitya Akademi, Trichur, 1996 (first published in 1932), p. 57.
49. K.M. Unnikumaran Nair, 'Samyamanathinte Gunangal', *Mathrubhumi*, vol. 22, no. 9, 23 July 1944, p. 1.
50. Where her height and complexion partly due to the fact that like some other Thiyyas of Malabar, English blood ran in her veins, is supposed to have made people mistake her for a Malabar princess!.
51. Partha Chatterjee, 'The Nationalist Resolution of the Women's Question', in K. Sanghari and S. Vaid, eds., *Recasting Women: Essays in Colonial History*, Kali for Women, Delhi, 1997, pp. 238-9. But the segregation between the public and the private spheres were not always complete. On the situation in Kerala, Devika writes that 'Partha Chatterjee's well-known argument regarding the fading of social reform (that called for state intervention) as a framework for addressing the Woman Question in India towards the close of the nineteenth century and the nationalist 'protection' of the domestic

domain as sacred 'innerspace' outside the purview of the modern state does not apply to Malayalee society of the early twentieth century. . . . In fact, it was precisely at this time that the state was called upon to legislate in order to transform the 'inner-most' social spaces, those of marriage and family by community movements whose major agenda was the transformation of internally-heterogeneous, loosely-structured pre-modern caste groups into internally homogeneous, strongly bound and mutually exclusive modern communities. J. Devika, 'Negotiating Women's Social Space: Public Debates on Gender in Early Modern Kerala, India, *Inter-Asia Cultural Studies*, vol. 7, no. 1, 2006, p. 46. However, except for such moments when the Western-educated middle class sought the help of the colonial authorities in bringing about changes in their marriage and inheritance systems which they saw as legacies of a barbaric past, generally, they were zealous guardians of the sanctity of their homes.

52. Kannippayyur Sankaran Nambuthiripad, 'Stri Svatantriyam', in *Unni Nambuthiri*, vol. 7, no. 4, 1926, p. 288. There were the odd counter-arguments, of course, coming mostly from educated women. It was, for instance, pointed out that 'women's slavery was due to their lack of economic freedom, and that so long as men continued to control the "keys to the money-box", women would remain like a monkey in the hands of a Kuravan.' Malati, 'Streekalum Udyoga Svikaranavum' *Murali*, vol. 1, nos. 7-8, March-April 1934, p. 62.
53. P.M. Manezhi, Antarjanangalum Avarude Vesha Bhushanangalum, *Unni Nambuthiri*, vol. 7, 1927, no. 12, pp. 714-16.
54. Bandhusamudayangalile Manya Sahodarikalodu Oru Apeksha, unsigned Article, *Unni Nambuthiri*, vol. 8, no. 12, 1928, p. 682.
55. Judith E. Walsh, *Domesticity in Colonial India: What Women Learned When Men Gave Them Advice*, Oxford University Press, New Delhi, 2004, p. 87.
56. C. Madhavi, 'Woman and Higher Education', *Government Brennen College Magazine*, March 1931, p. 45.
57. Ibid., p. 46.
58. By the late 1930s, the number of girl students even in the centres of higher education was quite significant. T. Narayanan Nambiar, while proposing the 'Toast of the College' twenty years after he had graduated from Government Brennen College, mentions how while he was a student there, 'we had very few girl students. . . . In those days we lived in two different worlds. But now I find the girl students

moving freely with boys and taking an active part in all the activities of the college.' T. Narayanan Nambiar, 'Toast of the College', *Government Brennen College Magazine,* vol. VIII, no. 1, December 1939, p. 84.

59. *Kerala Sanchari* 21 August 1889 in NNPR in the week ending 31 August 1889, p. 172.
60. Madhuravanam C. Krishna Kuruppu, 'Sahavidyabyasam', in V.R. Nayanar, ed., *Malabar Vidyabyasa Guide*, Mathrubhumi, Kozhikode, 1939, p. 49.
61. C.P. Govinda Pillai, Nammude Vidyabhyasa Rithi, *Gurunathan*. . . . However, there were cases of women doing exceptionally well in the field of higher education. E.K. Janaki, daughter of the sub-judge E.K. Krishnan, went on to graduate from Presidency College, Madras, and did her M.Sc. from Michigan University on a scholarship in 1926. 'Miss E.K. Janaki Ammal', unsigned article, *Mithavadi* Special Issue, 1927, pp. 43-4.
62. B. Bagirathy Amma, 'Chila Parishkara Udyamangal', *Mathrubhumi Weekly*, vol. 10, no. 5, 25 April 1932, p. 35.
63. T.C. Kalyani Amma, 'Stree Vidyabhyasam', *Mithavadi,* Special Issue, 1927, p. 46.
64. *Report on Public Instruction in the Madras Presidency for 1939-40*, vol. 2, pts. I and II, p. 51.
65. A Women's Education Commission appointed by the Nambudiri Yogakshema Sabha, in its report, recommended that if considerable number of *Illams* existed together, schooling could be organized in one of them, thereby denying the need for public schooling. Education was also to be limited to girls between five and twelve. Married women's education, meanwhile, was to be decided by their husbands. K.M. Sheeba, 'From the Kitchen to the Stage and Back: Continuing Forms of Women's Exclusion in Keralam', in *Journal of South Indian History*, vol. 2, no. 2, March 2006, p. 65.
66. K.P. Kesava Menon, *Kazhinha Kalam*, p. 23.
67. Diary of G. Sankaran Nair, dated 29 June 1925.
68. K.M. Nair, *Muliyil Krishnan*, Norman Printing Bureau, Calicut, 1932, pp. 36-7.
69. C.K. Revathy Amma, *Sahasra Poornima,* Vidyavilasam Press, Tellicherry, 1977, p. 28.
70. S. Menon Marath, *The Wound of Spring*, Malayalam trans. M. Gangadhara Menon, Poorna Publications, Kozhikode, 1997 (1st pub. 1960).
71. Bandhu Samudayangalile . . . , p. 682.

72. Kamala Das, *A Childhood in Malabar*, tr. Gita Krishnankutty, Penguin, New Delhi, 2003, p. 179.
73. Changarakumarath Sankaran, *C. Krishnan*, Sidhartha Book House, Trichur, 1967, p. 92. Others went further, and led a productive public life. C.K. Damayanthi Amma, the first woman social worker from these parts, set up a Ladies Club, and started a mobile library for its members. Her daughter C.K. Revathi Amma became a District Board member, and later wrote her autobiography, *Sahasra Poornima* which went on to win the Kerala Sahitya Akademi Award. But these were largely exceptions to a generalized picture where women stayed at home.
74. J. Devika, *Her-Self: Early Writings on Gender by Malayalee Women, 1898-1938*, Stree, Kolkata, 2005.
75. J. Devika, 'Negotiating Women's Social Space: Public Debates on Gender in Early Modern Kerala, India', *Inter-Asia Cultural Studies*, vol. 7, no. 1, 2006, pp. 48-51.
76. J. Devika, *Imagining Women's Social space in Early Modern Keralam*, CDS, Thiruvantahpuram, 2002, p. 9.
77. 'Sangeetavum Sahityavum', unsigned article in *Mathrubhumi Weekly*, vol. 10, no. 16, 11 July 1932, p. 5.
78. Panikkar, op. cit., p. 27.
79. V.V., 'Vasthradharanathe Patti', *Mathrubhumi*, vol. 19, no. 11w, 1 June 1941, p. 19.
80. Diary of G. Sankaran Nair, dated 21 December 1926.
81. Diary of K.P.S. Menon, dated 25 July 1923.
82. The Difference-Differal of a colonial modernity – Public Debates on Domesticity in British Bengal, in David Arnold, David Hardiman eds., *Subaltern Studies VIII, Essays in Honour of Ranajit Guha*, Oxford University Press, New Delhi, 1994, pp. 55-6.
83. Murkoth Kumaran, *Ammamarodu*, Kerala State Council for Child Welfare, Trivandrum, 1977 (1st pub. 1927), p. 11.
84. K. Narayani Kutty Amma, 'Keraliya Vanithakulum Avarude Innathe Kadamayum', *Mathrubhumi*, vol. 10, no.1w, 28 March 1932, p. 19.
85. C.V.K. Elayathu, Dambathiyathil Sugamundo Illayo . . . , p. 724.
86. M. Lakshmikuttyamma, Nambudiri Balikamarude Vidyabhyasam, *Unni Nambuthiri*, vol. 9, no. 1, 1928, p. 76.
87. Ibid., p. 81.
88. Ibid., p. 82.
89. Sanjayan, for instance, criticized women's talkativeness and obsession to control their husbands in works like 'Kamalathinte Kathu' and

'Bhartrujatha', Prabhakaran Pazhassi, *Sanjayan: Kalathinte Manasakshi*, Department of Cultural Publications, Thiruvanthapuram, 2000, p. 102.

90. Variath Balakrishna Menon, *Premabandham*, Durgalaya Press, Chittur, Cochin, 1917, pp. 1-2.
91. Chakravarty, op. cit., pp. 60-1.
92. N. Naryana Ilayathu,'Paurasthya Vanithakal', *Mathrubhumi Weekly*, vol. 10, no. 22, August 1932, p. 32.
93. Oru Bharathiya Vanitha, op. cit., p. 8. In London, K.P. Kesava Menon was shocked at the sight of inebriated women coming out of bars. K.P. Kesava Menon, *Bilathi Visesham*, p. 76.
94. Unsigned article, *Mithavadi*, vol. 3, no. 5, February 1916, p. 22.
95. Unsigned article, 'Bharthakkanmarude Vishamasthithi, *Vijayan*, vol. 2, no. 7, August 1938, p. 17.
96. P.M. Manezhi, 'Antarjanangalum Avarude Vesha Bhushanangalum', *Unni Nambuthiri*, vol. 7, 1102 (1927), no. 12, pp. 714-16.
97. Partha Mitter, *Art and Nationalism in Colonial India: 1850-1922: Occidental Orientations*, Cambridge University Press, Cambridge, p. 206.
98. Adrian Mayer, op. cit., p. 198.
99. Ibid., pp. 110-11.
100. C. Kesavan, *Jeevithasamaram*, DC Books, Kottayam, 2010 (1st pub. 1968), pp. 72-3.
101. M.P. Bhattadiripad (Premji), *Rhuthumathy*, Current Books, Trichur, 1991 (1st pub. 1944), p. 57.
102. The odd resistance may have come in the form of opposition by traditional family members. In a passage from a novel, which might be a reflection of society, Panchu Menon talks of how he has not tried wearing chappals ever since his uncle gave him a sound thrashing when, at a young age, he had tried putting them on. O. Chandu Menon, *Indulekha*, DC Books, Kottayam, 2010 (1st pub. 1889), pp. 64-5.
103. William Logan, *Malabar*, vol. I, Asian Educational Services, New Delhi, 1989 (1st pub. 1887), p. 134.
104. Murkoth Kumaran, *Vasumati*, Sriramavilasam Press, Kollam, 1935, pp. 1-2.
105. Ananda E. Wood, *Knowledge Before Printing and After*, Oxford University Press, New Delhi, 1985, p. 52.
106. Pradeep Bose, 'Sons of the Nation', in Partha Chatterjee, ed., *Texts of Power: Emerging Disciplines in Colonial Bengal*, University of Minnesota Press, Minneapolis, 1995.

107. N. Naryanan Elayathu, 'Pourasthya Vanithakal', *Mathrubhumi Weekly*, vol. 10, no. W22, 2 August 1932, p. 26.
108. Murkoth Kumaran, *Ammamarodu*, Kerala State Council for Child Welfare, Trivandrum, 1977 (1st pub. 1927), p. 22.
109. G. Raman Menon, 'Nammude Sthrikalude Sukhathinu Aavashyamaya Chila Karyangal', *Mitavadi*, vol. 3, no. 5, February 1916, p. 32.
110. Swapna M. Banerjee, 'Child, Mother, Servant: Motherhood and Domestic Ideology in Colonial Bengal', in Avril A. Powell and Siobhan Lambert-Hurley, eds., *Rhetoric and Reality: Gender and the Colonial Experience in South Asia*, Oxford University Press, New Delhi, 2006.
111. Murkoth Kunhappa, *Murkoth Kumaran*, Sahitya Pravarthaka Co-operatrive Society Ltd., Kottayam, 1975, p. 88.
112. Janaki Ram, *V.K. Krishna Menon: A Personal Memoir*, Oxford University Press, New Delhi, 1997, p. 4.
113. K.V. Moosathu, *Atmakatha*, National Book Stall, Kottayam, 1966, p. 41.

CHAPTER 3

Changing Forms of Leisure

In a passage from the biography of C. Krishnan, lawyer-turned-publisher, written by his son, we get a glimpse of a day in the life of the middle class in urban Calicut. Of his father's daily routine, Changarakumarath Sankaran writes:

> getting up at around 4.00 a.m, he goes for a morning walk (with a fur cap in the non-rainy season) which takes him up to the railway station, where, adjusting his watch according to the railway time, he moves along the beach up to West Hill from where he turns back home. After strolling in the garden for a while, he gets fresh, changes dress, and has his breakfast which includes one glass of milk, grapes, and dry fruits. This is followed by a stint in his nearby office from where he returns to take his afternoon bath followed by a sumptuous lunch consisting of six different curries including fish and meat. Back in office, writing letters engage him in the afternoons. Returning home in the evening, he eats some oranges and oats (after turning fifty, he never took dinner). In the evenings, he received visitors, of whom the most frequent was Ramayyar, the famous vakil in Malabar. After friends and acquaintances leave, he spends time with his family, and goes through newspapers and magazines including *Punch, Tit Bits, Modern Review, Times of India, The Statesman,* etc. as well as books, mostly non-fiction, available in his rich library. Finally, around ten he goes to sleep.[1]

This passage reveals, among other things, C. Krishnan's attempts to fix hours for everything ranging from the early morning walk up to the time he retires to bed, interspersed with space kept aside for leisure. Compared to the past when such segregations were rare, we find, during this period, the urbane middle class, following a busy schedule, and contemptuous of laziness, finding space, all the same, for leisure. As one writer put it 'while entertainment without purpose is like dead leaves, life without entertainment is like a tree without leaves.' Leisure was given its due importance in the life of the individual, and indeed, in some cases, its relevance as a serious topic of research was stressed. As was noted in the pages of *Malabar Quarterly Review*, one of the premier contemporary English magazines from these parts,

> It is not the serious side of man's nature alone that deserves our careful study. His games, his pastimes, his diversions . . . equally call for minute research. . . . For, there, the spirit, bereft of artificial conventionalities, runs riot in her perennial atmosphere, and shows herself in her true colours. It is in those happy moments of relaxation that the inmost virtues of man come out . . . relaxation repairs his weakened spirits and makes him the fitter to face the future struggle. . . .[2]

In the following pages, an attempt is made, from available sources, to unravel what constituted leisure for the middle class in colonial Malabar.[3]

* * *

According to Joffre Dumazedier, the French sociologist, leisure serves three main functions to the individual – relaxation, diversion and personality development.[4] Work is distinct from leisure. While the former is specific as well as predictable, the latter is not. But this was not the case earlier when there was hardly any distinction between the two. Leisure, according to Stanley Parker, was a product of industrial society. When work came to be done in a separate place, with specific timing and under special conditions, all of which were absent in earlier times, leisure got its new identity distinct from work.[5] George A. Lundberg defined leisure as 'the time we are free from the more obvious and formal duties which a paid job or other obligatory occupation imposes upon us'.[6] In more recent times, feminist scholars have rejected such a residual definition of leisure by pointing out that such an explanation fails to account for the unpaid labour women (both housewives and employed) perform at home in the form of child-rearing and housekeeping. For women, the private domestic space is not always a realm of non-work. Women have less time of their own after their household chores, whereas men's leisure activities get priority. Home, thus, becomes a gendered space reflecting the unequal relations that exist between men and women outside it.[7]

John Mcguire observes that in colonial India, leisure for the British ruling class meant a closed class activity revolving around ritualistic club life, whereas the *bhadralok* preferred to relax in traditional ways, most of which involved household activities.[8] The same could be said of the middle class elsewhere in the country.

In Malabar, in the late nineteenth and early twentieth centuries, under the impact of colonial modernity, changes occurred in the modes of leisure. Some among the middle class, recollecting a 'golden past', rued these changes, and fondly recalled an era when, for instance, during the Onam celebrations, 'people enjoyed new clothes, the feast, and games afterwards, where women, children and men participated' in contrast to the present where 'after the perfunctory meals, the husband takes a newspaper, and smoking a cigarette, settles down on his armchair.' Nostalgic and clearly at a loss in the new millieu, the same writer further pointed out that 'even watching drama on a reserved ticket, or eating out in Calicut at Modern Hindu Hotel and Kohinoor with all their modern amenities were poor substitutes to watching a traditional drama in the village or having idly and tea from a mess in the school days'.[9]

The above quote represents the anxiety and a feeling of loss experienced by quite a significant section of the middle class as colonial Malabar underwent dramatic social changes. But there were others who welcomed these changes. They pointed out how, for instance, in the past the institution of caste had prevented 'national' games where everybody could participate from developing in the region. As one writer commented,

> the institution of caste and its sentimentalism have isolated our national games and reduced us to the level of spectators rather than actors therein. . . . A Brahmin is interdicted if he trains himself up in feats with arms or athletic exercises. Nairs alone can exercise *Velakali* or sham fights, why? We have to seek the solution for all these enigmas in the disintegration of society by caste and the resultant deterioration.[10]

In earlier societies, leisure was not seen as distinct from religious activities. For instance, in Malabar, M.S.A. Rao points out that, in earlier times, women in old *tarawads* and *illams* spent their leisure hours in reading sacred lore.[11] This relation between leisure and religious activities in the past had been taken note of by early twentieth-century representatives of the middle class. Raja Raja Varma Raja observed how, formerly, most of the entertainment in the villages had a religious flavour:

> in fact religious occasions were the times for public entertainment. Some are religious observances, but partake the character of games.-*Utsavams, Bharani, Puram*, etc. . . . Yet, I cannot shut my eyes to the recreative element predominant in each. All games in history had religious origins . . . it is found impossible in several cases to determine clearly where the religious element stops and the secular element begins, or whether some festivals are to be classed under the head of games or religious experiences.[12]

Not that secular forms of entertainment did not exist at all in the past. They did, and some like hunting persisted well into the twentieth century. The terrain of Malabar, with its thick vegetation, was fit for wildlife, so much so they posed a threat to human lives. This was the context in which the colonial government rewarded hunters who shot dead animals like bear, leopards and elephants. The hunter had to provide evidence of the killed animal in the form of its teeth, tails, etc., which the authorities would consequently destroy so that they cannot be recycled.

Hunting or *nayaattu*, thus, had been a favourite pastime in the past. Following the birth of his son, Krishna Menon's father, Krishnan Kurup, the lawyer-son of the Raja of Kartanad is said to have celebrated the occasion with a round of hunting which lasted days.[13] M.P. Sivadasa Menon, in a highly readable work, through anecdotes and stories, describes in great detail the different facets of hunting in colonial Malabar.[14] Hunting brought forth immense joy to its votaries. 'First with bows and arrows,' a connoisseur observed, 'and then with rifles and pistols, native hunters bagged his game, and with it, a spirit of self reliance in dangerous situations and a sense of pleasure in difficulties overcome.'[15] In an appendix to Dunsterville's Railway souvenir, an account of the wildlife in parts of Malabar and the possibilities of hunting are given:

[at Walayar] you are in the middle of the finest jungle imaginable. This is the place from where the Station-master sent the now almost classic telegram, 'Tiger dancing on platform, please arrange.' I myself have often seen the pugs of a tiger on the platform, and the pointsmen have or had iron-based gates to their watch-boxes. Formerly people were escorted through this part of the jungle along the high road by guards and tom-toms to keep off the elephants, which even in my time have come close to the station. Along this portion of the line, all sorts of animals may be seen, and on one occasion, one of the engineers saw a tiger carry off a pig, which was on the side of the line, and jump over the hedge with it whilst the train was passing. Engine drivers have shot panthers from their engines and it was altogether a paradise for sportsmen. So far as tigers are concerned there are still a good many to be found, but the country is not adapted for beating, and it is only by chance you come across them. . . . There are still, I have no doubt, plenty of bears to be had. . . . Their caves are within a few minutes' walk of the station, and time was when I have killed a couple and been back at Podanur in time for breakfast. . . . From Calicut the crocodile can be hunted along the Beypore river and the Kuddeelundi backwater, this, combined with other shooting may be enjoyed from a boat and is the ne-plus ultra of luxurious sport. . . . The last time I stood on the Railway bridge of this river or backwater, I counted no less than four crocodiles basking on the mud banks, two of them, of which I shot one, were about 9ft. in length.[16]

With the emerging middle class turning their back on the past, hunting, which, though considered a secular pastime, lost its shine as it was too closely associated with the feudal culture of the past. Colonial forest laws ensured that it would, at best, remain the exclusive privilege of a few native and foreign elites.[17] Of what was once a favourite sport, one native writer lamented:

with the development of the modern idea of property in land, the forests ceased to be regarded as 'terra naturalis' and began to be gradually enclosed; the financier stretched his greedy hands amidst these untouched spots and reserved them for public purposes; the servants of the *sirkar* enforced the game laws and protected the monopolies. All these added to the spread of ever-increasing population opening up new habitations and pastures, has cooled the very embers of the enthusiasm in such exciting and active games.[18]

With hunting as a pastime going out of vogue, the search was on for new forms of physical entertainment. There was a growing realization, during this period, of the importance physical activities play in the well-being of the individual, and, consequently, the community. Research has shown how in Victorian England, the importance of physical activities, which was believed to enhance physical and mental well-being, was stressed.[19] A similar attitude is in evidence in contemporary literature in Malabar. For example, it was pointed out that 'mental health depends on physical health. . . . Physical exercise strengthens the muscles, purifies blood, expands the brain, and ensures good health . . . helps an energetic ideal man to live long.'[20] 'Physical education', it was, similarly, argued, 'does not stop with mere muscle-building. It is concerned with rational, normal growth and development, with vitality, with health, happiness, efficiency and character.'[21]

Critique was directed against the way education was imparted to children without avenues for physical activities. Referring to the military style discipline in schools complete with time-bells and drill system, an article in *Gurunathan* argued that 'it was high time to change the educational system which, instead of allowing time for children to play and for exercises, confined and controlled them within the four walls of the classroom'.[22] Alternative schemes of education where physical exercises would be given their due were proposed in several forums. It was argued that 'a modern programme of health and physical education . . . by providing opportunities for boys and girls for wholesome living . . . can make a distinct contribution both to the individual and community life'.[23] It was felt that physical training should start early on in life. According to K.K. Nair,

> the deterioration of the physique among the educated Indians, is entirely due to their perfect indifference to school games during the early part of their scholastic career. . . . The school games when properly conducted are invaluable aids to students for the development of their physical strength . . . as, after a hard day's mental labour in the class, the student surely finds it a great relief to play a game at football, Tennis or Cricket in the evening.[24]

Apart from physical well-being, exercise was also believed to improve the moral well-being of the participants, instilling in them 'those grand moral qualities such as patience, perseverance, pluck and self-denial without which a nation can never excel in anything'.[25] Murkoth Kumaran observed that 'playing cricket with passion would lead to selflessness . . . and a good cricketer will become a good citizen'.[26] The middle-class discourse was particular in making a distinction between exercise and labour as the latter was believed to be something in which the lower classes excelled in.[27]

Several games mushroomed in Malabar during this time. Facilities for games like table-tennis and carrom as well as billiards which were becoming popular during this time were provided by the various clubs which mushroomed all over the region.[28] School authorities were 'encouraging students to participate in games like badminton, tennis, volleyball, hockey, football, and cricket which do not even have equivalents in the Malayalam language'.[29] In some cases, well-to-do families had these facilities even at home. V.K. Krishna Menon's parents, who were also good chess players, had a billiards table at home. Once, Krishna Menon's father tried to get his rather studious son to play billiards, but after his careless son spoilt the green on the table, the attempt was abruptly called off.[30]

Among spectator-sports, cricket soon acquired pre-eminence. Although the region was to produce players of international stature only much later, in the popularity stakes, it was second to none. Cricket, in these parts, had a long history, longer, in fact, than many other regions which, over time, acquired a stronger tradition in the game. The Tellicherry Cricket Club, for instance, was formed in 1860.[31]

Matches were organized involving both the whites as well as the natives.[32] Weekend matches were played at Mananchira maidan in Calicut where clubs from Tellicherry, Palghat, Kannur as well as distant Ceylon and Mangalore participated. Cricket was then still a gentleman's game. Murkoth Ramunny writes how during the inter-town matches, the Canannore players used to carry dried fish for their counterparts in Coorg, and the favour would be returned when, during the return match, the Coorg team would bring down to the plains, oranges.[33] The growing popularity of cricket is reflected in the following passage taken from an article aptly titled 'The Craze for Cricket':

> Cricket is very much in the air now-a-days. You hear every second man you meet doling out his unwanted opinions about the 'King of Games'. I have noticed even clerks from Government offices . . . talking about spins and late-cuts. Once, cricket was the passion of a few atheletes. Now it has developed into a fashion of society. If you cannot pass verdicts upon Merchant's century or Mankad's spins, you are a complete wash-out in social circles . . . earlier the craze was films. . . . Today, the cream of society is more interested in Hafeez's hair-cut or Nimbalkar's eyebrow.[34]

With an increase in time for leisure and interest in it, holidays and the growth of amusement industries became widespread. Modern drama made its appearance in Malabar during the early twentieth century, under colonial influence when English plays were translated and staged. But, generally, there were no good local troupes, and it was the visiting Tamil troupes that made a lot of money in this region. Of the few Malayalam dramas that got staged in the early twentieth century were T.C. Achyuta Menon's *Sangheeta Naishadam*, *Saranjani Parinayam,* and *Sadaram*. Later, the Kottakal Arya Vaidya Sala was to play an important role in the promotion of the indigenous theatre tradition in the region. In 1909, was set up its theatre wing, Paramavilasa Nataka Company, with the training of its members taking place near the Vaidyasala building. Among its contributions was the translation of *Sakuntalam* into a Malayalam musical drama. Performances took place all over Malabar and even Cochin and Travancore. At Calicut, it had its own hall – P.S.V. Hall – where dramas were staged until in 1924, when the Health Department prohibited public functions there. With the advent of cinema, drama was to lose its popularity. The latter, its tickets more expensive to begin with, took 5-6 hours to finish, while cinemas would take no more than 3 hours, and the tickets were cheaper. Consequently, in October of 1939, 'Parama Vilasa Nataka Sangham' became PSV Natya Sangham with the emphasis now shifting to Kathakali.[35]

The period also witnessed the emergence of a new art form – *Kathaprasangam* – a combination of the earlier tradition of story-telling and political speeches of the new era. This was to become very much part of the progressive movement, and was especially strong in the southern part of the state. However, the public entertainment which really captured the imagination of the public was motion picture which made its appearance in Kerala in the 1920s. By the middle of the century, it was observed that 'almost all the towns have one or more permanent theatres' while in the villages there existed 'temporary or touring talkies which people would travel miles to watch'.[36]

Long before the first full length movie was screened in Kerala, its prototype made a tentative beginning in Malabar. In 1913, with a projector he acquired from an engineer in Thirichirapally, Jose Kaattukaran showed movie clips of events including the 1906 earthquake in Chicago to those who bought tickets ranging from Rs. 2 downwards. The venue for the touring cinema, Jose Electric Bioscope, often would be maidans and paddy fields in Kozhikode and its periphery. As for cinema, initially, Malabar, like the rest of the state would be flooded by Tamil and Hindi language movies. It was only in the late 1930s with movies like *Balan* that Malayalam cinema came into its own. Before that, there were mostly Tamil melodramas coming from across the border.[37] And even the few early Malayalam movies were heavily influenced by their Tamil counterparts. As an observer pointed out, 'these films had nothing to do with Kerala in their content except its landscape of coconut groves and lakes'.[38] During the silent phase of cinema, language was not a barrier as a person used to announce what was happening on screen as he saw it. During the intervals, to keep people interested, there would be clowning, music and dance, ingredients, all of which would later be incorporated into mainstream cinema. Initially, before cinema houses made their appearances, screenings used to take place in the open air or tents with the aid of low-cost projectors. As movies caught the imagination of the public, several cinema halls came into existence, sometimes at the expense of theatres where earlier dramas used to be enacted. In 1925, 'Radha' came up with a seating capacity of 1300, with separate enclosures for women and female employees to usher them in. 'Crown' which came up later used to screen English and other foreign language movies mainly to cater to the European audience in the town.[39]

Cinema had become a craze for the Malayalis. Nothing else could match its entertainment value. As a student in his school magazine put it, 'to escape from the hubbub of this tumultuous world, to forget our miseries, it is better to visit the theatre [cinema hall] than the liquor shop or the gambling den'.[40] Murkoth Kunhappa noted that 'in every bookstall, you will find film magazines, and in every nook and corner, people reading them, and singing film songs'.[41] In the same article, he continued – 'after the advent of the movies, almost everyone wants to become a film hero or heroine. Seeing the wealth they make, and fame and adoration they enjoy, it is not surprising.'[42]

In Tamil Nadu, during the corresponding period, a movement led by Lakshmikantan's magazine, *Cinemadhoo*, attacked films from a moralistic viewpoint stressing how the medium was destroying long-held values in society. A parallel movement in Kerala is not in evidence. Instead, commentators in contemporary magazines pointed out how in spite of its drawbacks, caused mainly by the involvement of uneducated people seeking quick profits in the making of films, its utilities, especially educative content, far outnumbered them. As one put it, 'Cinema . . . has various uses, the most important being educational. . . . By watching one or two movies, we Indians can learn more about the traditions and customs of the English than possible by reading many books.'[43] It was argued that 'if the objective of art was to provide man with both happiness and idealism, then there is no cheaper art form available than cinema'.[44] The medium's progressive possibilities, its moralizing lessons, were also highlighted. For instance, it was pointed out that 'the stories depicted in Shantaram's *Sakuntala* and Prakash pictures' *Ramarajyam* show women can survive without depending on men, which is a blow to those who argue women should go back to the kitchen'.[45] Another commentator observed that if the film *Mathrubhumi* stresses the importance of an educated agrarian class and the use of technology in cultivation, *Devdas* moralized against alcoholism.[46]

Kerala, especially Malabar, had a rich tradition of circus, Tellicherry providing the earliest and best artistes in this field. Of all those associated with circus in the state during the colonial period, Keeleri Kunhikannan was the most famous. Born in Tellicherry in 1858 to a Thiyya family, Keeleri had very little formal schooling.

During his youth, he used to watch E.N. Overbury, an English official, organize gymnastics at the Tellicherry maidan. In 1884, he saw a circus for the first time in Madras. In 1887, Vishnupant Chatre's circus came to Kerala, and Keeleri had the opportunity to interact with the legendary Maharashtrian. It was these experiences which propelled Keeleri towards a career in circus. He soon learnt the horizontal bar, parallel bar, Roman rings, etc., with his *kalari* and wrestling background, no doubt, helping.[47] From 1884 to 1932, he served as the physical instructor of BEMP School in Tellicherry. During this time, he was able to effectively combine his official work with his passion. He had set up in his hometown a Circus Training School, which provided training to future artistes. One of his disciples, Kannan Bombayo made a mark in Europe as well as the USA, impressing, among others, Adolf Hitler who supposedly called him the 'Jumping Devil of India'.[48] In the early twentieth century several circuses sprang up in Malabar – the Pariyali's Malabar Grand Circus, the Great Raymon Circus, the Great Bombay Circus, etc. With the animals, jokers, and, of course, the performing artistes, circus had a great attraction in those days to the burgeoning middle classes who flocked to these shows on holidays with their kids. Age was not a bar, because as one of the advertisements went, 'once you enter the tent, even an old man becomes a child'![49]

In early twentieth-century Malabar, thus, as theatre, cinema, circus and sports flourished, a new audience was created. These were not like the private artistic performances held in the past inside the homes of the rural rich where the spectators would be confined to family and caste members. As long as one had the money to buy tickets, entry was ensured.

Meanwhile, with the advancement of transport, it became possible to travel beyond one's own immediate locality. E.M.S. Namboodiripad recounts in his memoirs his first trip outside Kerala, a pilgrimage to Rameswaram, where the long train journey, inspection of tickets by officials, food from outside, staying in hotels – all new experiences – proved immensely thrilling.[50] But, travels now included not just the pilgrimages to Guruvayur and elsewhere but also included tours for sheer pleasure. The railways were to play an important role in facilitating this newfound mobility. The hero of

Indulekha could traverse Calcutta, Bombay, and of course, Madras, because of the railways. Train journey left lasting impressions on the first-timers. During the poet, Balamaniamma's first train journey to Kolkata, she found 'the light and crowds in each station very interesting' and which reminded her 'of a Tamil drama troupe camping at my village and their dramas in childhood'.[51]

Students' magazines reveal how in schools and colleges, such tours tried to combine study with the pleasures of picnic. After one such excursion to Tiruvilwamala, a junior intermediate wrote 'camp life is indeed the most pleasant life imaginable. It is full of enjoyment and full of lessons for us'.[52] Among the spots chosen for tours and picnics in Malabar, the green forest of Wynad was one of the most popular. After vividly describing the forests, plantations and the exotic tribals in the area, the Kurumbas in particular, one traveller, returning from such a visit, concluded – 'I venture to suggest that a trip to this beautiful place will be very useful for those who had not the good fortune to enjoy the beauties of nature'.[53] S.K. Pottekkatt, one of the better-travelled writers to have emerged from Malabar, in a travelogue piece describes the exotic locales and tribes he came across during a trip he undertook to the Nilgiris in 1942.[54]

By the early twentieth century, there was a class of middle-class individuals who had to travel for education and employment to different cities. In the case of a lucky few, England became the destination for higher education. These were mostly middle-class men who could afford to travel, or else had state patronage to conduct these travels. They, unlike the workers who also travelled to distant areas but could not pen their experiences, had the necessary skills to do so. This was the conjuncture when the Malayalam prose had matured, literary magazines were proliferating and betterment of transport facilities made travels possible, that travelogues emerge in the vernacular.[55] Travel-writing along with photos of the places visited became common in the issues of various magazines. Amongst the earliest of the travelogues – and one of the most popular as well during this time – was *Bilathi Visesham* authored by K.P. Kesava Menon, who travelled to England for the first time in July 1912. This work which was first published in 1916, and went through several reprints thereafter, was an account of his stay in England. Though

Kesava Menon, like others of his ilk, tries to distinguish between an Indian way of life and the west in an unconscious effort to define the self, generally, as Simonti Sen points out in her work, most of these early travellers went to England with pre-conceived notions, their ideas of England already formed during their school days.[56] For instance, one wrote of how he 'had been reciting English poems and reading English stories from childhood . . . [and] while setting out for England, had the hope of seeing for real the places described there.'[57] In many cases, it was these 'Grand tourists' who, after returning to India, defined and re-fashioned 'taste' among the natives.

Earlier, there had been little requirement for hotels. Now, the need to work outside one's own hometown, official visits to other cities, tours for pleasure, all combined to create a necessity for restaurants and lodges which sprang up in towns like Tellicherry and Calicut. They were, as somebody put it, 'well furnished with modern equipments and elegant system of service, novel in their names and their sign boards'.[58] Eating out with families became common during this time. Going in the evenings to the beach along with relatives or friends was another pastime indulged in by the middle classes.

New goods had become available from the late nineteenth century. The need was felt to keep a minimum standard of existence, for, the British had made it out that a society's civilizational status could be determined by its material progress, comforts and conveniences available. Shops selling specialized consumer items became a feature of these towns, the advertisements in the pages of magazines like *Mathrubhumi* revealing the kind of goods in demand for a growingly consumerist middle class society. The new goods ranged from toilet soaps, hair oils, aphrodisiacs, clocks, toys, suits, to motorbikes. Shops in the cities were different in appearance from those in the villages 'with big sign boards, attractive names, beautiful display of the products sold, salesman and saleswomen in uniform, and showcases displaying the things for sale'.[59]

Another major constituent of leisure during this time was reading, especially novels. K.N. Panikkar observes that the emergence of the novel was rooted in the intellectual needs and aesthetic sensibility of the burgeoning middle class.[60] Similarly, Shivarama Padikkal argues that the novel was an entirely new genre, arising from the historical moment when the English educated middle class was attempting to imagine a modern nation.[61] Early novels in the Malayalam language beginning with *Indulekha* enjoyed colossal success. With the growth of individualism, reading too had taken an individualistic turn. In earlier times it was a collective enterprise. The growth of the private domain and changes in the nature of enjoyment ensured that reading now took place at home individually. The reverse was also true-reading promoted individualism, as Rhys Issac argues. Regular reading, he says, produced 'modes of silent thought' generating, in the process, 'individualism'.[62] The emergence of the novel reflects this transition best.

In earlier times, leisure was not seen as something distinct from religious activities. For instance, in Malabar, as M.S.A. Rao points out, women in old *tarawads* and *illams* spent their leisure hours in reading sacred lore.[63] Religious literature continued to have its fans even in the twentieth century. For instance, in the novel *Premabandham,* Devikutty reads out Puranas and stories of mythical heroes to her daughter Amukutty.[64] Churia Canaran, who went on to become the deputy collector of Malabar, spent his leisure hours in reading Sanskrit works, especially those devoted to theology and philosophy.[65] But these instances were becoming rare as religious poetry based on the epics gradually gave way to secular prose in the popularity stakes.

Even as novels and other forms of fiction took their rightful place in the reading world of the newly emergent middle class, critiques were produced against popular novels by some middle-class intellectuals. Vengayil Kunhiraman Nayanar made fun of intending novelists who were proliferating in an article titled 'Akhyayika Allengil Novel'.[66] Ramankutty Menon wrote a novel titled *Parangodi Parinayam* which was a parody of the immensely popular *Indulekha* as well as a critique of modernity.[67] These critiques were prompted partly due to the male middle class fear that reading novels might develop base instincts and corrupt the readers, especially women. A critic pointed out that 'in most of the novels, which, in their wisdom, textbook committees prescribe for young students, there are vivid descriptions of the amorous activities of love-lorn couples . . . if only the talents of these writers are used for narrating the biography of great men which would set the right example for young minds.'[68] As Tapti Roy says, in India, initially, the colonial regime categorized the press and defined what is obscene and what is not. Later, it was left to the indigenous elites to define what was 'proper' and 'improper' in literary aesthetics.[69]

Before the advent and popularization of electricity, evenings were spent in darkness. In his account, Mayer wrote that in many parts of the district, 'lighting is made possible using coconut oil lamps, or lanterns of kerosene oil; electric power exists only in the largest towns'.[70] But that did not prevent those who were swept off their feet by the printed word from devouring books by daylight. For example, Sanjayan, the famous satirist, during his childhood used to rush home from school and before the sun went down, read his favourite *Bhaktamala* authored by Tharavathu Ammalu Amma.[71] Sukumar Azheekode who later went on to acquire fame as orator-writer-academician writes of how in his childhood, his reading habit got a boost through his father's library which, according to him, contained more books than some of the public libraries around![72]

That the middle class had taken seriously to reading is clear from the diary of G. Sankaran Nair, a lawyer and a congress activist who regularly used to read, apart from Malayalam magazines like *Mitavadi* and *Prabudha Keralam*, English newspapers like *Times of India*, *The Hindu* as well as *The Modern Review* published from distant Calcutta. Sanjayan was an ardent reader of *Punch* from young days as well as *Tit-Bits*.[73] Often, members of the middle class subscribed to more than one magazine, and, in some cases, even foreign ones. Kamala Das, the famous poetess, recalls how, while in Calcutta, her father used to get the British *Daily Mirror*, and the American weekly *Saturday Evening Post*, and while staying at her village in Malabar, he used to subscribe to *Manorama, Mangalodayam, Parijatam* and *Mathrubhumi*.[74] Men, since they were more literate and had better access to the public sphere and, therefore, kept track of literary and cultural developments, had a wider range of periodicals to choose from, but women were not altogether kept out of the process. Kamala Das, for instance, talks in her memoirs of how she was an avid reader of the weekly-love stories of Uroob and Pottekkat, and used to enjoy solving puzzles which appeared in the magazines.[75] One periodical the middle class in these parts could identify with was *Mathrubhumi*. Beginning with articles and short stories, it soon had different sections on children, women, science, gardening, literature, cinema, etc., alongside its regular commitment to nationalist politics. A.R. Venkatachalapathy has shown how, in the context of Tamil Nadu, the magazines, as a new business tactic, indulged in a successful mix of humour, crossword puzzles with fabulous prizes, cartoons, fiction with its thrills, suspense, melodrama, and passed them under a new legitimizing label – nationalism.[76]

★ ★ ★

One evening sometime in early 1927, at Kozhikode, a big crowd assembled at the house of an engineer, K.C. Menon to listen to a radio broadcast from Bombay. But the evening ended in utter disaster and the engineer cut a sorry figure when no sound emanated from the radio set. The explanation given by the engineer, that it was the inclement weather that was to be blamed, cut no ice with those who had bought tickets, and money had to be refunded. Radio, thus made a tepid beginning here, but within a few years would become one of the most popular household item.

Amateur broadcasting had begun in the country in the 1920s, and radio clubs had sprung up in the big cities like Calcutta, Bombay and Madras. The Indian Broadcasting Company, set up in 1926, tried to cash in on what it thought was a growing demand for the new marvel and sponsored the establishment of regular radio stations. But very few subscribed, and the company had to be closed down. In 1935, the government entered the field and set up the Indian State Broadcasting Service which later got renamed as All India radio in 1940.[77] Apart from five stations in the princely states, by the early 1940s, it had six radio stations across the country. Radio, with its staple of music, news and sport commentary, soon became extremely popular, and by the time, India gained Independence, the number of people who had radio licenses had risen to 248,000.

In Malabar, during the first half of the twentieth century, the initially bulky and expensive apparatus was not very common, and in the smaller towns and villages, it was almost unknown. Even as late as 1939, 'Ottapalam had only one [a battery-operated] radio set in its only club'.[78] Those who could not afford it, listened to the radio at restaurants and other public places, while others took refuge in their rich neighbour's house. In late 1933, one girl recalled in the pages of *Mathrubhumi,* the excitement she felt while listening to music from the radio of her doctor neighbour who had invited her family over in the evening.[79] Radio programmes included music, news, weather report, market fluctuations, etc., and had a wide audience. Of radio's significance, one commentator observed: 'Only twenty years have elapsed since its inception. But during this short period it has assumed such marvelous proportions that today it has almost become a household necessity . . . only problem is its prohibitive cost . . . the government should do something.'[80]

By the middle of the twentieth century, there was the widespread use of radio.[81] M.S.A. Rao writes, 'with the invention of the wireless, gramophone has become less popular. For the people who can afford to possess a set, it is the chief mode of spending one's leisure. As it caters to different interests (music, songs, news, lectures, plays and sometimes religious programmes) it has come to be considered as a necessity of a home.'[82] Many people who could not afford it, listened to the radio in public places, restaurant and parks. In Calicut, for instance, there was a big transistor radio placed at the Mananchira square where people in the evenings used to come and listen.

We have already seen the interest shown by the middle class in decorating the interior of their homes. If a spurt of interest in maintaining flower gardens is any indication, they were equally concerned about how the house looked from the outside. The fiction of the times is replete with gardens adorning middle-class homes. In *Vasumati*, for instance, Murkoth Kumaran begins the story with the description of a garden with marble statues, fountain and benches belonging to a well-off Thiyya.[83] The coming into being of nucleated families living in separate homes enabled people to work out their botanical fantasies. The vegetable garden which partly fed the family continued to exist, but the new craze was for the flower garden which soon became a symbol of middle-class status. Appreciating flower gardens has been traditionally seen as a feminine attribute, but there is no evidence for that in contemporary literature. Members belonging to both the sexes recognized in equal measure the aesthetic pleasures they offered, and the health benefits one stood to gain while working in them. The following passage from a college magazine is a case in point:

> a flower garden is a veritable paradise on earth. It has a charm of its own. A beautiful garden in front of a home or a public institution is indeed a delightful sight that welcomes the visitor . . . Gardening . . . besides giving exercise to the muscles, provides an interesting and useful pastime for one's leisure hours. Ministering to the dumb colourful plants and flowers in the open air, inhaling the sweet scented air, is sure to add to physical as well as mental growth and refinement.[84]

The middle classes, in order to distinguish themselves from the lower orders, avoided menial labour at any cost. But there was no such taboo as far as garden tending was concerned.

* * *

It is not, though, always possible to distinguish between leisure partaken at home and those available outside it. In many cases, as in certain kinds of games, as well as music, there is an overlap. Similarly, talking was an important pastime, traversing both home and outside. 'Talking,' according to Nels Anderson, 'is the most universal of pastimes, and also quite the cheapest, in our society . . . it has its place in every society. To be exiled from it, as when prisoners are put into solitary confinement, often leads to madness. It enables one to identify with one's social milieu.'[85] Dipesh Chakravarty writes of the institution of *adda* in colonial Bengal which, as a legacy of an earlier period, persisted in spite of Victorian reservations regarding it as against the values of modernity. It was believed to confirm the 'laziness' of the natives and hinder family life. In spite of such reservations, *adda* in the coffee houses, parks and beaches helped one to feel at home in the epoch of modernity, providing a democratic space – though women were conspicuous by their absence – the discussions not having any telos, no conclusion, and no agenda.[86] This was the period when 'taste' was gaining in prominence in middle class life, the capacity to discriminate beauty and perfection in art and literature. The art of conversation, the ability to express the opinions gained through appropriate reading marked out the 'cultured' from the rest. The talking sessions were facilitated by the proliferation of friendships, similar professions and common public interests bringing people together. Kamala Das writes that her uncle's friends including advocates, literary figures, diplomats, and physicians would turn up at their home in the evenings and have conversations on the verandah, and that when the discussions got heated and lasted long, some stayed back overnight.[87] Visiting homes of people with similar background and interests had become popular. P.S. Variar of Kottakkal Arya Vaidya Sala fame was 'a great host', his biographer notes, 'and entertaining guests was like a hobby to him'.[88] By the early twentieth century, the institution of caste no longer had the prohibitory effect it had earlier in restricting public interaction between members of different castes and, as shown in the next chapter, the period threw up several close friendships between the Nairs and the Thiyyas.

A relevant question in this context is whether leisure and work are inherently incompatible. H.L. Wilensky distinguishes between two types of people – those who try to compensate for the frustrations they experience while at the work place through leisure, and others who look for similar experiences during their leisure time to those they experience while in the office. While the former holds true for those whose working conditions are harsh, the latter refers to those whose work is interesting and requires a certain amount of skill and education.[89] Among the latter, would be examples from the middle class. O. Chandu Menon, the famous novelist who combined his literary work with a career in the judiciary, is a case in point. On reaching home after settling a difficult case, he would relax at home by making his servants take sides in a mock case, occasionally joining in himself.[90] On other occasions, during office hours, after his superiors had left for home in the late afternoons, he would indulge in songs and dance with friends.[91]

The anxiety of the middle class in keeping a distance from both the decadent feudal culture of the past as well as the sensibilities of the lower orders determined the ways in which they enjoyed them. For instance, when an educated elite took to Mohiniattam, a medieval dance form, it was in its sanitized *avatar*, devoid of its erotic content. In the 1930s, under Vallathol's leadership, the Kerala Kalamandalam, had sanitized Mohiniattam through, among other things, the segregation of the female dancer from the accompanying male artistes, and by the introduction of more refined instruments like *mridangam*, flute and fiddle which replaced drums. The *devadasi* system, to which the dance form had links was banned. This was not an exception but was, instead, a pattern that marked the cultural scene across the country in the first half of the twentieth century. As Sumit Sarkar, in the context of nineteenth-century Kolkata, observed, 'Victorian notions of respectability and Puritanism enforced by official censorship and elite *bhadralok* pressure, largely destroyed the rich plebian culture and condemned it as obscene and licentious'.[92] Similarly, even as the middle classes flocked to cinema halls along with the multitudes, they ensured that they would be seated in the higher-priced sections separately from the masses. A morally upright middle class also made public their reservations regarding those who were associated with the medium, a stigma which has persisted over the decades. This was the era when society was getting democratized, and when the masses gained access to cultural forms, whether it was reading novels, which the expansion of printing had helped to proliferate or going for a musical concert or an art exhibition. The elites, by defining good taste, ensured that literature and painting got segregated into the 'good' and the 'bad', which ensured the hierarchization of culture into the 'high' and the low, the masses progressively getting alienated from the former as it became more and more abstract and difficult to comprehend. To sort of institutionalize this segregation, there was the creation of associations and clubs to which the lower classes had no access. Social segregation, by now, had come to be based on class. Caste hierarchies of an earlier generation, though not totally erased, hereafter would exert less influence as the next chapter will demonstrate.

NOTES

1. Changarakumarath Sankaran, *C. Krishnan*, Sidhartha Book House, Trichur, 1967, pp. 65, 74-6.
2. M. Raja Raja Varma Raja, 'Our National Games', *The Malabar Quarterly Review*, vol. III, no. 3, September 1904, p. 158.
3. Sources are scarce on this topic, a problem not peculiar just to Malabar. While discussing leisure in nineteenth-century England, Walton and Walvin refers to the problems a researcher faces including the lack of documentation for pre-industrial and early industrial leisure forms (the little there is having been done by disapproving contemporaries), the problems in assessing the sexual and class nature of audience at spectator sports, as well as the difficulties involved in describing the informal use of free time of individuals / families outside commercial / institutional context, especially within home. John K. Walton and James Walvin, eds., *Leisure in Britain: 1780-1939*, Manchester University Press, Manchester, 1983, pp. 3-4.
4. Joffre Dumazedier, *Toward a Society of Leisure*, translated by Stewart E. McClure, New York: Free Press, 1967, p. 16. Some scholars differentiate between leisure and recreation. The latter has a moralistic tinge to it, intending to reform the individual. This had its origins in early industrial societies including England where, under the influence of Christianity, the idleness of (especially) the working class was considered a social threat. Thelma McCormack writes, 'Recreation is a system of social control, and like all systems of social control, it is to some degree manipulative, coercive and indoctrinating, leisure is not.' Thelma McCormack, 'Politics and Leisure', *International Journal of Comparative Sociology*, vol. 12, no. 3, September 1971, p. 168.
5. Stanley Parker, *The Sociology of Leisure*, London: George Allen & Unwin Ltd., 1976, p. 27.
6. George A. Lundberg et al., *Leisure: A Suburban Study*, New York: Columbia University Press, 1934, p. 2.
7. Betsy Wearing, *Leisure and Feminist Theory*, London: Sage, 1998; Rosemary Deem, *All Work and No Play?: The Sociology of Women and Leisure*, Milton Keynes: Open University Press, 1986.
8. John Mcguire, *The Making of a Colonial Mind: A Quantitative Study of the Bhadralok in Calcutta, 1857-1885*, ANU Monograph on South Asia, no. 10, Australian National University (1983), p. 77.
9. A.C. Govindan, 'Annum Innum', *Mathrubhumi Weekly*, 1934, 26 March, vol. I, no. 12, p. 8.
10. M. Raja Raja Varma Raja, op. cit., p. 262.

11. M.S.A. Rao, *Social Change in Malabar*, The Popular Book Depot, Bombay, 1957, p. 179.
12. M. Raja Raja Varma Raja, op. cit., pp. 159-61.
13. Janaki Ram, *V.K. Krishna Menon: A Personal Memoir*, Oxford University Press, New Delhi, 1997, p. 2.
14. M.P. Sivadasa Menon, *Malabarile Sikkaru*, DC Books, Kottayam, 2002 (1st pub. 1959).
15. M. Raja Raja Varma Raja, op. cit., p. 225.
16. 'Smooth-Bore', 'Sport in Southern India', appendix in F. Dunsterville, *Illustrated Guide to the Madras Railway*, Madras, Higginbotham and Co., 1898, pp. 92-3.
17. However, wild animals remained a menace for human settlements in Malabar. The *Manorama* commented that earlier, the hunting expeditions of the *maharajas* saved people from wild beasts, and, now, in the changed circumstances, revenue officers on circuit should do the same. *Manorama*, 31 January 1913 in NNPR for the week ending 8 February 1913, p. 255. Meanwhile, the 'unofficial' shooting down of wild animals when they became a threat to human populations, continued. The *Kerala Patrika* reports that 'one Vattiyil Muhammad Kutti, the *Adhikari* of Kutilangadi, shot two tigers last Sunday, and that he has altogether bagged 31 tigers.' It goes on to add that 'a European was appointed during Sir Arthur Lawly's governorship to shoot wild animals' and 'a small pay granted to men of Muhammad Kutti's stamp will go a long way in the destruction of wild animals and protection of cattle and cultivation from their ravages.' *Kerala Patrika*, 10 February 1912 in NNPR for the week ending 17 February 1912, p. 264.
18. M. Raja Raja Varma Raja, 'Our National Games II', *The Malabar Quarterly Review*, vol. IV, no. 1, March 1905, p. 225.
19. James Walvin, 'Children's Pleasures' in John K. Walton and James Walvin, eds., *Leisure in Britain: 1780-1939*, Manchester University Press, Manchester, 1983, pp. 228-229.
20. P.S. Namboodiri, *A Handbook of Physical Activities*, Mangalodayam Press, Trichur, 1935, pp. iii-iv.
21. Ninan Thomas, 'Physical Education: What & Why', *Government Brennen College Magazine*, March 1931, p. 31.
22. P.R. Neelakantan Nair, 'Nammude Vidyabhyasam', *Gurunathan*, vol. 6, no. 1, Chingam, 1927, p. 8.
23. T. Paul Joseph, 'The Scope of Physical Education in Schools', *The Teachers' Magazine*, Journal of the Cochin Teachers' Association, vol. XV, nos. II and III, 1941, p. 55.

24. K.K. Nair, 'The Importance of Physical Training in Schools and Colleges', *Zamorin's College Magazine*, vol. I, no. I, August 1912, p. 18.
25. Ibid., p. 19.
26. Murkoth Kumaran, 'Vidyarthikalude Vinodakalikal', in O.V. Abdulla, et al., eds., *Vishwabhanu*, Mathrubhumi Publishers, Calicut, 1936, p. 158.
27. Boria Majumdar has traced the gradual evolution of passion for physical games among the educated middle classes in colonial Bengal. In the beginning, the educated middle class remained aloof from all kinds of sporting activity. While games like cricket and football were looked down upon as exclusive European preserves, indigenous sports like wrestling were confined to the lower classes. Between 1800 and 1860s, the *bhadralok* patronized indigenous sports like wrestling, though they did not themselves participate in such activity. They organized competitions in which their servants fought against each other amidst great excitement and enthusiasm. It was in the 1870s and 1880s when charged with effeminacy that the educated Bengali middle classes strove to integrate sporting activity, rooted in physical culture into their everyday lives. Boria Majumdar, 'A Case of Indian Exceptionalism: Bengali Middle Class Patronage of Sport in Colonial Bengal' in Sanjay Joshi, ed., *The Middle Class in Colonial India*, Oxford University Press, New Delhi, 2010, pp. 281-2.
28. For instance, the SNDP club started at Calicut in 1912 by C. Krishnan provided facilities for table-tennis, carrom, etc., to its members. Sankaran, op. cit., p. 33.
29. Kumaran, op. cit., p. 156.
30. Janaki Ram, op. cit., p. 2.
31. The legend has it that, while staying as an official of the East India Company in Malabar, Arthur Wellesley used to organize cricket matches on the shores involving those who came for trade to the sea coast. According to another local tradition, when Colin Cowdrey's father, E.A. Cowdrey, came to Coorg as an administrator of estates, he used to frequent Tellicherry, from where his son learnt the basics of batting while taking on the bowling of his butler, Raman. During the first world war, an exhibition match was organized at Tellicherry to collect funds for the war efforts.
32. Several examples are there. To cite one, a cricket match was organized between Basel Mission College and Oxford and Bucks Light Infantry on third November, 1911 at Calicut. *BGM College Magazine*, Calicut, vol. III, no. 1, July 1912.

33. Murkoth Ramunny, *Thalasserry: Sarada Krishnayyar Memorial Fine Arts Society Smaranika*, Chitra DTP Solutions, Tellicherry, 2002, p. 141.
34. P.N. 'The Craze for Cricket', *Zamorin's College Magazine*, vol. XIX, no. 1, August 1947, p. 39.
35. Keezhedath Vasudevan Nair, *Vaidyaratnam P.S. Variar*, P.M. Variar Managing Trustee, Kottakal, 1953, p. 102.
36. Rao, op. cit., p. 182. Calicut, for instance, had two cinema halls – Coronation and Crown, while Tellicherry had on its four borders, 4 theatres – Mukund, Venus, Lotus, and Prabha.
37. The three Malayalam movies before 1947 were *Balan* (1938), *Jnanambika* (1940), and *Prahlada* (1941).Thirunilath and Joseph, ed., *Kerala Film Directory*, Joseph and Co., Cochin, 1956, p. 243.
38. Nagavally R. S. Kurup, 'Malayala Chithrangulude Bhavi', in Thirunilath and Joseph, ed., *Kerala Film Directory*, Joseph and Co., Cochin, 1956, pp. 79-80.
39. Chengaattu Gopalakrishnan, *Chalachithra Vyavasaayam Keralathil*, Chintha Publishers, Thiruvanthapuram, 2013.
40. Ummer C.O.K., 'The Talkies', *BEMP School Magazine*, April 1941, p. 16.
41. Murkoth Kunhappa, *Cinema*, The Mangalodayam Ltd., Trichur, 1951, p. 1.
42. Ibid., p. 35.
43. 'Cinema Allengil Chalachitram', unsigned article, *Mangalodayam*, 1917, cited in *Pachakuthira*, vol. 1, no. 5, December 2004, pp. 55-6.
44. Pottekkatt Achyuta Menon, 'Cinema Athava Chalanachithram', in *Murali*, vol. 1, no. 6, February 1934, p. 29.
45 Vidvan P.R. Varyar, 'Chalachithravaum Chaaritrarakshayum', *Mathrubhumi Weekly*, vol. 22, no. 33, 5 November 1944, p. 8.
46. S. G. Nair, Vidyabhyasavum Cinemayum, *Mathrubhumi*, vol. 19, no. 35, 16 November 1941, p. 24.
47. Sreedharan Champad, *Circusinte Lokam*, Mathrubhumi Books, Kozhikode, 2008, p. 129.
48. Murkoth Kumaran. 'Sriman Keeleri Kunhikannan', *Mathrubhumi Weekly*, vol. 11, no. 38, 11 December 1933, pp. 4-5.
49. Kantampulli Balan, *Circus*, Sahitya Parishad Cooperative Society Ltd., Ernakulam, 1961, p. 44.
50. E.M.S. Namboodiripad, *Atmakatha*, Chintah Publishers, Trivandrum, 1985, p. 61.
51. Balamaniamma, *Jivitathilude*, Mathrubhumi Printing and Publishing Co. Ltd., Kozhikode, 1969, pp. 68-9.

52. K.C.A..M., 'Our Excursion', *Zamorin's College Magazine*, March 1938, vol. X, nos. 1 & 2, p. 49.
53. K.G.K. Nair, 'Wynad', *Zamorin's College Magazine*, October 1938, vol. XI, no. 1, p. 38.
54. S.K. Pottekkatt, 'Neelagiriyilekku Orullaasayaatra', *Ente Vazhiyambalangal*, Poorna Publications, Kozhikode, 2008, pp. 54-65.
55. K. Satchidanandan, 'Travel Writing in India: An Overview', in Shobhana Bhattacharji, ed., *Travel Writing in India*, Sahitya Akademi, New Delhi, 2008, p. 3.
56. Simonti Sen, *Travels to Europe: Self and other in Bengali Travel Narratives, 1870-1910*, Orient Longman, New Delhi, 2005.
57. B.K., 'Ente London Yathra', *Mathrubhumi*, vol. 23, no. 32, 21 October 1945, p. 2.
58. Rao, op. cit., p. 58.
59. Ibid., p. 59.
60. K.N. Panikkar, 'Creating a New Cultural Taste: Reading a Nineteenth Century Malayalam Novel', in *Culture, Ideology, Hegemony: Intellectuals and Social Consciousness in Colonial India*, Tulika, New Delhi 1995, p. 96.
61. Shivarama Padikkal, 'Inventing Modernity: The Emergence of the Novel in India' in Tejaswini Niranjana, P. Sudhir and Vivek Dhareshwar eds., *Interrogating Modernity: Culture and Colonialism in India*, Seagull, Calcutta, 1993.
62. Rhys Issac, *The Transformation of Virginia (1740-90)*, Chapel Hill, North Carolina, University of North Carolina Press, 1982, p. 122.
63. Rao, op. cit., p. 179.
64. Variath Balakrishna Menon, *Premabandham*, Durgalaya Press, Chittur, Cochin, 1917, p. 17.
65. E.K. Krishnan, 'A Brief Account of the Life of the Late Mr. Churia Canaran, Deputy Collector of Malabar', *The Malabar Quarterly Review*, vol. III, no. 3, September 1904, p. 29.
66. Vengayil Kunhiraman Nayanar, 'Akhyayika Allengil Novel', in *Kesari Nayanarude Krithikal*, Mathrubhumi Printing and Publishing Company Limited, Calicut, 1987.
67. Kizhakkepattu Ramankutty Menon, *Parangodi Parinayam* (1892), in George Irumbayam, *Naalu Novelukal*, Trichur, Kerala Sahitya Akademi, 1983.
68. P. Sukumaran, 'Novelukal', *Dharmaprabha*, vol. 1, nos. 5-6 (August & September 1933), p. 167.
69. Tapti Roy, 'Disciplining the Printed Text', in Partha Chatterjee, ed.,

Texts of Power: Emerging Disciplines in Colonial Bengal, Minneapolis: University of Minnesota Press, 1995.

70. Adrian C. Mayer, *Land and Society in Malabar*, Bombay: Oxford University Press, 1952, p. 108.
71. Prabhakaran Pazhassi, *Sanjayan: Kalathinte Manasakshi*, Thiruvanthapuram: Department of Cultural Publications, 2000, p. 17.
72. Sukumar Azhikode, *Azheekodinte Athmakatha*, DC Books, Kottayam, 2010, p. 23. He also adds that the fact that he came from a learned family ensured recognition from his upper caste neighbours.
73. Pazhassi, op. cit., p. 74.
74. Kamala Das, *A Childhood in Malabar*, tr. Gita Krishnankutty, Penguin, New Delhi, 2003, pp. 106-7.
75. Ibid., p. 107.
76. A.R. Venkatachalapathy, 'Domesticating the Novel: Society and Culture in Inter-war Tamil Nadu', *The Indian Economic and Social History Review*, vol. XXXIV, no. 1 (January-March 1997).
77. G.C. Awasthy, *Broadcasting in India*, Bombay, Allied Publishers, 1965, pp. 2-3.
78. P.K.S. Kutty, *Years of Laughter: Reminiscences of a Cartoonist*, Thema Kolkata, 2009, p. 51.
79. Sumangaladevi, 'Akashavani', *Mathrubhumi Weekly*, vol. 11, no. 39 (18 December 1933), p. 24.
80. K. Chintan, 'Radio', *Zamorin's College Magazine*, vol. XI, no. 1 (October 1938), pp. 4-5.
81. In the post-Independence period, the government consciously promoted the use of radio. According to an analyst, this was for two reasons: the need to speak directly to a huge population of illiterates, and to preserve the cultural–literary tradition of the region. K.M. Narendran, 'Kozhikode Akashavani' in *Malabar: Paithrukavum Prathapavum*, Mathrubhumi Books, Kozhikode, 2011, pp. 535-6.
82. M.S.A. Rao, op. cit., p. 183.
83. Murkoth Kumaran, *Vasumati*, Sriramavilasam Press, Kollam, 1935, p. 257.
84. S. Sooryanarayan Iyer, 'Our School Garden', *Zamorin's College Magazine*', vol. XI, no. 1 (October 1938), pp. 21-2.
85. Nels Anderson, *Man's Work and Leisure*, E. J. Brill, Leiden, 1974, p. 94.
86. Dipesh Chakravarty, 'Adda: A History of Sociality' in *Provincialising Europe: Post-Colonial Thought and Historical Difference*, Princeton University Press, Princeton, 2007, pp. 180-213.

87. Kamala Das, op. cit., pp. 15-18.
88. Keezhedath Vasudevan Nair, *Vaidyaratnam P.S. Variar*, P.M. Variar Managing Trustee, Kottakkal, 1953, p. 164.
89. H.L. Wilensky, 'Work, Careers and Social Integration', *International Social Science Journal*, vol. 12 (1960), p. 544.
90. Ambramoli Kunhiraman Vaidyar, 'Rao Bahadur O. Chandu Menon F.M.U.', *Mitavadi*, vol. 5, no. 4 (1913), p. 12.
91. Murkoth Kumaran, *Oyarath Chandu Menon*, Kerala Sahitya Akademi, Trichur, 1996 (1st pub. 1932), p. 46.
92. Sumit Sarkar, *Modern Times: India 1880s-1950s*, Permanent Black, New Delhi, 2015, p. 304.

CHAPTER 4

Caste and the Middle Class

In late colonial Malabar, at the new workplace and in the public arena, the earlier legitimacy enjoyed by caste got eroded. Privileges based on birth counted for less; instead, evaluating an individual based on his internal values gained prominence. People began to give up their caste-markers which, in an earlier era, had helped people identify different castes and behave accordingly in a highly hierarchized society. The new middle class, a product of the socio-economic changes brought about by the British, was at the forefront of these changes. As Andre Beteille says:

> The whole idiom of purity and pollution which was the cement as it were of the old social hierarchy is antithetical to middle-class modes of life and work. It is impossible to organize work in a modern office in conformity with that idiom. Social exclusion on grounds of ritual defilement, if practiced consistently, will bring to a standstill the work of any modern institution, whether a bank, a laboratory or a newspaper. For all its many sins, it was the middle class that first grasped the significance of this and took the initiative in discrediting the rules of purity and pollution.[1]

This may have been so. But, as this chapter seeks to show by examining contemporary literature, the vestiges of the past persisted in the minds of a few, and at a deeply personal level, caste continued to play a significant role.

A Social Order based on Caste Hierarchy

In 1930, when the British government nominated C. Krishnan, a Thiyya, as a representative of the Madras Legislative Council, it must have been the crowning moment in an already illustrious career. Krishnan had, by then, completed successful stints as an advocate, banker and publisher. His wife was running an Ayurvedic shop from home, whose products were in demand even abroad. And his subordinates in the office included several upper castes, some of whom were Brahmins. Around the same time, another Thiyya, Keeleri Kunhikannan, the circus artiste from Tellicherry was enthralling audiences around the state. His disciples, at least one of whom went on to attain fame in Europe, included castes lower to him. This was all a far cry from the scenario at the turn of the century when interaction between the castes was at a premium prompting Swami Vivekananda to dub the state a 'mental asylum'!

Caste inequities had been exceptionally severe in Kerala, with practices of untouchability and unseeability making life intolerable for the lower castes. Even up to the early twentieth century, caste barriers, though no longer as strong as in the past, prevailed. The time for the abolition of untouchability, and entry for the lower castes into temples still remained distant. Those among the middle class who had their early education in the villages remembered how caste played a determining role in their everyday lives. For instance, Thikkodiyan, who went on to acquire fame as a radio broadcaster and dramatist, writes of how in the village school he attended in the early part of the twentieth century, upper caste boys like him were segregated from the lower castes, and how the master, in order to avoid pollution, would not beat a low caste student, but instead would throw the stick at him from a distance![2] C. Krishnan recounts how, while at Madras Presidency College, the college canteen maintained two rooms for upper castes from Kerala, where the lower castes including Thiyyas were not allowed. He, along with others, drew the attention of the principal to this problem, following which, a separate room was kept aside for the Thiyyas and others.[3] It is not as if the lower castes were always at the receiving end. C.H. Kunhappa, editor of *Mathrubhumi*, and a Nair himself, talks of how numerically dominant Thiyya boys in Tellicherry during his school days used to make fun of Nair students, calling them, among other things, 'Nairkutty Naikutty' literal translation of which would be 'Nair children are puppies'.[4] Inspite of interaction between the castes in a newly-emergent public sphere, interdining between them took a long time in coming. Mozhikunnath Brahmadattan Namboodiripad, a rare Hindu hero of the Malabar Rebellion writes in his memoirs of his excommunication by the community for having indulged in interdining during political work.[5] Casteism remained institutionalized amongst the Indian officials in the colonial bureaucracy. On 31 September 1906 *Vivekodayam* condemned the Town magistrate of Calicut, Gopala Krishna Ayer who, in the open court, observed that a Thiyya who had not got out of the way of a Nair on the road was 'lucky [that he was] not killed' and that 'such people deserve to have bones of their body broken'.[6]

The lowest castes and tribes in the period we are discussing did not leave much written sources behind, making it all the more difficult to reconstruct their stories. In this context the small monograph written by A.V. Anil Kumar on the life of Yiramyav is important. Incidents from his life make it abundantly clear how tough life for them was then. In one instance, when plague was creating havoc in the area, the white plantation owner set fire to a stable along with two tribal slaves who were staying there because two dead rats were found! He also talks of the custom where lower castes would be buried alive inside bunds separating fields because it was thought that the blood and sweat of human beings helped strengthen the bunds![7]

Overcoming the Distinctions of Caste

Impact of colonialism with its concept of equality before law, and indigenous reform movements led to the decline of caste in Malabar by the turn of the twentieth century.[8] Adrian Mayer, writing in the middle of the twentieth century, mentions how through education in schools, new occupations have been thrown open to Malayalis in administrative, industrial and commercial capacities in urban areas, the jobs offered not dependent on the the applicant's caste.[9] Missionary activities and the coming into existence of factories, where there was free mixing of castes, weakened the hold of Brahminism on society. It is not argued that caste disappeared overnight. Far from it. With regard to marriages and interdining at home, among other things, the institution took a long time in breaking down, and, in many ways, still linger on. But what is evident from contemporary sources is that as an institution in preventing social interaction there was a clear undermining of its role. Mayer talks of an occasion when a low caste Nayadi walked up and talked without embarrassment while he was with a Brahmin, only for the latter to comment later that such a thing could not have happened a few years ago.[10] Caste got modified during this period in accordance with the contemporary requirements in society. In an urban milieu among the middle classes in Malabar, as elsewhere in Kerala, ways were found to overcome the distinctions of caste facilitating an interaction between the different castes in the public arena, without which even the possibility of grouping them into a class becomes fraught with difficulties.

Gaining access to higher education, and consequent employment in the government service had been one of the means through which the lower castes, especially the Thiyyas, had acquired social mobility. Malabar Christian College at Calicut and Brennen College in Tellicherry had been in the forefront in providing higher education to the lower-castes. The Zamorin's College in Calicut, later renamed Guruvayoorappan College, for a long time, remained a preserve of the upper castes. Alongside lower-caste attacks on this institution for its casteist policies, there were misgivings expressed by even some high castes regarding the continued discrimination the Thiyya community had to face with regard to admission in spite of their economic progress. In a letter to *Mitavadi*, the Thiyya newspaper, one Brahmin was to write: 'Of all the difficulties in the way of Hindu progress, none deserve our attention more than the refusal to admit Tiyyans, a highly respected class into the Zamorin's college. . . . Those who take pride in the refusal of admissions are violating the most sacred of relations among the Hindus themselves.'[11]

In the early twentieth century, associations like the Samudaya Bahishkarana Sangham set up by K.P. Gopalan, a Thiyya congressman, tried to weaken caste feelings by boycotting those who held caste prejudices and to encourage interdining between members of different castes. There were some upper caste social activists as well who were involved in such movements. A Gaud Saraswat Brahmin, Lakshmana Surendranatha Prabhu, a public prosecutor in north

Malabar, as well as a freedom fighter, who had once led a hunger strike at the Tellicherry Saraswat Temple demanding equality in worship, organized interdining at home.[12] Taboos concerning eating habits were being dismantled. Mayer observed that 'with increased travel, many caste members find it impossible to prepare and eat food in the traditional manner at all times, and this trend has been reinforced by the general weakening of caste sanctions'.[13] Recently introduced beverages like tea and coffee on which traditional taboos did not exist were widely used during meetings and get-togethers. One reform-minded Nambudiri, writing in defence of these changes, wondered 'how one would find in the *Sruti Smritis* instructions whether Brahmins can have such things as coffee, tea, and soda lemonade which did not exist in those days, and whether to interact with today's new and numerous castes'.[14] Once in Kozhikode, when the Brahmin government *vakil* M.S. Ramakrishnayyar got the 'Rao Bahadur' title, he organized a dinner for officials and prominent citizens at Edwards Victoria Hotel, catered by a Thiyya, Panangadan Sanku. The journalist, Murkoth Kumaran could not help taking a dig at the turn of events. In *Kerala Sanchari*, Kumaran wrote that the newly decorated Rao Bahadur had, by hosting a party for the beef-eating Englishmen, whose leather-chappals desecrated the cowdung floors, with one shot, given a blow to the fortress of time-honoured customs and traditions which even the British guns had found difficult to conquer![15]

In the earlier times, the upper castes had zealously tried to maintain the division of labour based on caste and to prevent any possibility of admixture of blood between the different castes. In Kerala, due to the extreme level of untouchability and unseeability practised, it was imperative to distinguish the caste of the body at the very sight itself. And, as a consequence, for the different castes, there were identity markers which included the wearing of dress, ornaments, and even hairstyle. According to B. Rajeevan, 'the style of clothing, the shape and position of the tuft of hair and the differing styles and materials of the ornaments functioned as the caste marks of the bodies. The clothing of Malayalees up to the beginning of the 20th century was not primarily related to the sense of nakedness of the body.' Clothing functioned as a sign system to designate the caste of the body.[16] According to Mayer, 'formerly all upper castes of both sexes wore a simple white cotton cloth round the waist and reaching to the ankle (*mundu*), and a folded cloth thrown over the shoulder or across the chest. Tiyyans and others were not supposed to wear clothes below their knees . . . and were forbidden the shoulder cloth . . . if they violated these rules, they were beaten up and their houses burnt.'[17] Even the style of conversation indicated the superior/inferior status of the different castes. A Nair while conversing with a Nambudiri described his house as 'rubbish heap', food as 'old kanji (porridge)' while the food of a Nambudiri was termed as nectar.[18]

In twentieth-century Kerala, there were efforts to give up caste-markers. If in the south, attempts along those lines, following calls by Ayyankali – who exhorted the *pulayas* to give up their stone necklaces which distinguished them as low – had been marked by violence on the part of the upper castes, in Malabar where the caste rigidities were relatively milder under direct colonial rule, they were smoother. In some cases, the upper castes consciously parted with their caste markers, notably, *kuduma* (long hair on the head tied in a knot). If Madhavan, the hero of *Indulekha,* written in 1889, still clings on to his *kuduma,* by the 1920s, many had got rid of it. K.P. Kesava Menon, the Congress leader, recollects in his memoirs how while studying in Madras, he removed his *kuduma*, as a consequence of which, when he came back home, his father gave him a thorough scolding.[19] Staying away from home, it seems, provided the protagonists with the necessary freedom to break free of the caste shackles. E.M.S. Namboodiripad, cites the occasion when he and friends collectively got rid of theirs – a virtual *kudumamuri prasthanam* (movement to get rid of *kudumas*) – while leading a hostel life in Trichur during their college days.[20] This was followed by a *Poonool pottikkalprasthanam* (movement to get rid of the sacred thread), whereby the sacred thread was broken and burnt by E.M.S. Namboodiripad and eleven of his friends.[21]

In effect, Kerala society, under the dual impact of colonial modernity and indigenous reform movements had turned its back on external factors or exteriority in determining one's status in society. Instead, interiority was emphasized. What was novel in early twentieth-century Kerala was re-interpretation of human beings as a biological species which could be proved by rational scientific empiricism. Sree Narayana Guru, for instance, combined ideas of egalitarianism with science, as when, during his encounter with Gandhi who had reservations in the total elimination of the institution of caste, famously told the latter that the semen from any human male can impregnate any human female. 'These arguments', according to Caroline Osella and Filippo Osella 'are essentially modern in their appeal to an essential inner essence, to an empiricism which eschews appearance for positivist examination of reality, and to the triumphal authority of experimental proof'.[22] Love between couples belonging to different castes, at least theoretically, was encouraged. As the principal of Zamorin's College, in defence of love marriage, put it, 'the heart should decide. Caste, religion, *Smartha Vicharam* and astrology cannot restrict love between man and woman'.[23] In practice, the odd intermarriages like the one between the author of the novel, *Sukumari,* Joseph Muliyil, a Thiyya convert to Christianity and a converted Antarjanam (Nambudiri woman) did take place. Similarly, C.H. Kunhappa talks of a love marriage involving different castes at Brennen College during his intermediate days.[24]

The erosion of caste hierarchy and inequities, at the symbolic level, was made possible partly through what M.N. Srinivas has called 'Sanskritisation'. In Kerala, the best example of such an attempt would be Sri Narayana Guru's plan of action implemented by the SNDP Yogam which included elimination of superstitions, blood sacrifices, and worship of evil gods which were to be replaced by worship in temples, introduction of schools and libraries, industry, commerce and modern means of agriculture, frugality, and cleanliness.[25] Mayer observed that 'even as many high caste folk now take meat, though often in private or at hotels, some Thiyyas and Pulyas have turned vegetarian, by preference or in imitation of the higher caste habits'.[26] Sanskritization was reflected in marriage rites as well with the Thiyyas now including 'the sacred fire as witness of the marriage vows, a Brahmin rite not previously followed by them' and the Pulayas resorting to 'exchange of rings, tying of the tali thread and the mutual garlanding of the couple as additions to their old rite of exchange of clothes'.[27]

In an urban milieu, thus, caste identities in public life got eroded. The Thiyya spiritual leader Vaghbhadanandan attracted upper caste disciples.[28] Among the new middle class, friendships cutting across caste lines became common, similar professions and common public interests bringing them together. By the 1930s and 1940s, in certain educational institutions, especially ones in the north like Government Brennen College, caste was not very much a feature of campus life. A young girl, Gladys Ambat, in her 'Response' to the 'Toast of the College' in 1939, observed how 'Caste system and class distinction are practically unknown within our college walls. Students mix freely with one another'.[29] The period threw up several close friendships between the Nairs and the Thiyyas in spite of the trenchant caste hierarchy. Murkoth Kumaran, a prominent Thiyya literary figure, while staying at Tellicherry, was a friend and neighbour of K.T. Chandu Nambiar, a well known criminal lawyer as well as a leading literary critic. Regarding literature, they had their differences which they made public through their respective columns in the leading magazines of the period. Later, Murkoth and Nambiar started separate newspapers – *Katora Kutaram* and *Ramabanam* respectively – where they continued their literary dispute, which, however, did not, in any way, affect their friendship. Infact, Chandu Nambiar was Murkoth's *Shashtipoorthi* celebration committee's chairman, reading out his *Mangalapathram* on the occasion.[30] As G. Arunima points out 'sharing the same literary space created a community of intellectuals with at least one shared concern – of engaging with the experience of modernity that was shaping and often, confusing them'.[31]

There were other instances as well. Murkoth Kumaran, a good friend of Chandu Menon, the famous early Nair novelist of Kerala, was to later write a biography of the latter in which, he writes of his subject's close friendship with E.K. Krishnan, another prominent Thiyya of Tellicherry, 'it was only natural that both of them being accomplished, honest and innocent, they would get attracted to each other. While Krishnan was a natural scientist with a keen interest in plant and animal life, Chandu Menon was an expert on human affairs, caricaturing their faults and exalting their qualities. Both were interested in hunting'.[32] Similarly, the Thiyya, C. Krishnan, a former lawyer before turning to business and publishing, had a number of upper caste friends like Sir C. Sankaran Nair, Sir M. Krishnan Nair and Dr T.M. Nair. His secretary, for some time, was Anantaramayyar, a Brahmin. There were upper castes like Thelappurathu Narayanan Thampi and Koyippilly Parameswara Kurup who acted as sub editors in *Mitavadi*, a predominantly Thiyya magazine C. Krishnan brought out. In fact, his closest friend was Manjeri Sundarayyar, one of the prominent Brahmin *vakils* of Malabar who used to frequent the former's house in the evenings. In 1917, when the acting collector, J.A. Thoran, under pressure from the Zamorin, had banned the Thiyyas from using the approach road to the Tali Temple, the two friends had travelled together in Krishnan's horse cart, and along with Madhavan Nair and others, broke the said law, and threw the offending signboard into the nearby pond.[33]

Lingering Legacies of an Unequal Past

Following secularization and Westernization, caste and religion did not disappear from the soil of Kerala overnight. Instead, they took new forms like the caste associations. According to M.N. Srinivas, the birth and proliferation of caste associations in modern India was a consequence of the modern adaptation of traditional caste forms, with Western instruments of modernization like colleges, books, pamphlets and journals being utilized to create communal or caste consciousness.[34] The first significant articulation of the demands of the people of Kerala was not on the basis of any segment but holistic – in Travancore, for instance, initially, the natives had organized themselves as Malayalis to protest the dominance enjoyed by the migrant Tamil Brahmins in government services through the Malayali Memorial of 1891. But, later, it gave way to a segmentary approach, each part agitating for its particularistic demands – the Ezhavas who set up the SNDP Yogam in 1903, and the Nairs who gave shape to the NSS in 1914 forming separate caste associations to put forth their demands separately. In 1896, the Ezhavas had already submitted the Ezhava Memorial. This, then, was the rather tortuous road taken by a hierarchized society to attain a semblance of democracy and egalitarianism – communal road to a secular Kerala, in the words of George Mathew.[35]

But, the caste associations aiming to protect caste interests were more of a southern phenomenon, mostly active in Travancore – Cochin, the princely states where appointments to government services were more arbitrary than British Malabar, though the branches of the SNDP Yogam and the NSS could be found in the northern parts of the state as well.[36] Significantly, there was no equivalent of the Ezhava Memorial in Malabar – no Thiyya Memorial, for instance. Having said that, however, caste feelings persisted well into the twentieth century in Malabar as well. In spite of the public expression of friendships across caste faultiness, and the all too infrequent inter-caste marriages, a genuine breaking down of the caste barrier, especially at the personal level, still remained a distant dream. Dilip Menon, in his provocative essay on E.M.S. Namboodiripad, argues that even communism did not help the latter overcome his upper caste bias while reconstructing Kerala's past.[37] Murkoth Kumaran is said to have confided in private his anguish that his good friend O. Chandu Menon, in his first and most famous novel, *Indulekha*, did not include as a character a single Thiyya, a community numerically dominant, and by then educated and gainfully employed.[38] That all was not well is indicated by a few events in the lives of some of the characters we saw above. The biographer of Muliyil Krishnan, one of those Thiyyas who 'made' it, having become, among other things, a teacher at Presidency college in Madras, recounts how Nair friends of Krishnan used to say good things about him on his face, while pouring scorn on him behind his back, and how they would take food from his home, but would be wary of others coming to know of it![39] One incident shows how material success did not always ensure respect for the lower castes. Once, during Onam celebrations organized by the Malayali Club in Madras, while prominent Malayalis in the city were being felicitated on stage, all except Krishnan were garlanded.[40] When Churyayi Kanaran, a Thiyya, who went on to become a Deputy Collector at Ponnani, was appointed as Head Munshi, his Nair superiors harassed him, giving him only a mattress to work on, instead of a chair, prompting H.V. Conolly, the Collector, who had appointed him, to intervene on his behalf.[41] Though caste differences were not publicly acknowledged, at a subtle level, caste feelings got played out in the organizational structures, meetings and functions of the clubs the Malayalis gave shape to in Madras. According to Susan Lewandowsky who has worked on the Malayali population in Madras during the colonial period, the Thiyyas resented the dominance exerted by the South Malabar Nayars in the Kerala Club – where even refreshments would be first served to the latter – and gradually drifted to the more 'subaltern' Kerala Samaj.[42]

The ultimate destinies of the two characters we saw earlier – C. Krishnan and Keeleri Kunhikannan – would help put things in perspective. Caste inequities had been a concern for C. Krishnan from his college days in Madras, where, as we had seen earlier, he, along with others had fought against caste discrimination in the hostel mess. Later, he had been involved, while in Calicut, in violating, along with his upper caste friends, the restrictions on lower castes to use the Tali temple approach road. Ironically, he ended up converting to Buddhism, which would suggest that he never felt quite comfortable with his Hindu identity, where, in spite of his material success and public fame, he continued to occupy a lower position in the caste hierarchy. Similarly, we find the egalitarian, democratic illusions regarding caste Keeleri Kunhikannan had upheld in his youth falling by the wayside towards the end of his life. Keeleri, who had married a Vannan woman, trained lower caste disciples, and joined the Brahmo Samaj, found, to his utter dismay, that no Hindu was willing to marry his daughter as his wife belonged to a caste lower than his! Ultimately, Keeleri had to take refuge in Christianity.[43] A classic case of a man representing the ideals of modernity going down under the weight of the dark forces unleashed by tradition, some might say, at first glance. However, as the next chapter would show it was in slightly more complex ways than that the two ideas, not always antagonistic, played out on the soil of colonial Malabar.

NOTES

1. Andre Beteille, 'The Social Character of the Indian Middle Class' in Imtiaz Ahmad et al., eds., *Middle Class Values in India and Western Europe*, Social Science Press, New Delhi, 2002, p. 83.
2. *Thikkodiyan, Arangu Kanatha Nadan*, DC Books, Kottayam, 2008, p. 24. Through a reading of the autobiographies of people like R.K. Narayan, M.S.S. Pandian observes that upper castes who came under the influence of colonial modernity showed a marked reluctance to talk about caste as if 'to talk about caste as caste would incarcerate one into a pre-modern realm', and, instead, throughout the narrative the institution masquerades as something else. M.S.S. Pandian, 'One Step Outside Modernity: Caste in the Middle Class Imaginary', in Sanjay Joshi, ed., *The Middle Class in Colonial India*, Oxford University Press, New Delhi, 2010, p. 241. However, in Malabar, R.K. Narayan's Malayali counterparts, especially those who came under the influence of Left-radical movements are more forthright in describing their experiences in relation to caste.
3. Changarakumarath Sankaran, *C. Krishnan*, Sidhartha Book House, Trichur, 1967, p. 5.
4. C.H. Kunhappa, *Smaranakal Matram*, Mathrubhumi Press, Kozhikode, 1981, p. 76.
5. Muzhikunnathu Brahmadathan Namboodirippad, *Khilafath Smaranakal,* Mathrubhumi Books, 2010 (first published in 1965), pp. 143-51.
6. *Vivekodayam*, 31 September 1906 in NNPR for the week ending 31 September 1906, pp. 346-7.
7. A.V. Anil Kumar, *Yiramyav: Atimayude Jeevitham,* Mathrubhumi Books, Kozhikode, 2009.
8. There is a vast literature on Caste system in India In the 1960s, Louis Dumont, in his highly influential work, highlighted the significance of caste in Indian society, which for him, was a feature from the earliest times. Louis Dumont, *Homo Hierarchicus: The Caste System and its Implications*, University of Chicago Press, Chicago, 1980. However, critique of Dumont appeared in the 1970s and 1980s where it was pointed out that a rigid caste system as well as the stereotypical Indian village were very much colonial constructs. Cohn, for instance, wrote, that 'in some sense it might be argued that the British created the Indian village' and that 'they rigidified some groups and institutions, which formerly had been contingent and flexible' such as castes. Bernard Cohn, 'Is there a new Indian History?

Society and Social Change Under the Raj', in *An Anthropologist among the Historians and Other Essays*, Oxford University Press, New Delhi, 1970, pp. 195-6. Nicholas Dirks has argued how, during the colonial encounter, following censuses, Gazetteers, etc., caste became the sole basis of one's identity subsuming others. Nicholas Dirks, *The Hollow Crown: Ethnohistory of an Indian Kingdom*, Cambridge University Press, Cambridge, 1987. In the context of Kerala, Muralidharan has argued that the modern forms of community came into existence in Kerala during the colonial period as a result of British administrative policies, Christian missionary activities and socio-religious reform movements. M, Muralidharan, 'Hindu Community Formation in Kerala: Processes and Structures under Colonial Modernity', *South Indian Studies*, 2, July-December 1996. In more recent times, the extreme views have given way to a more balanced approach to the institution of caste. Bayly, for instance, holds the view that both the old idea of timeless India and the newer revisionism which almost claims that colonial administration made India into a caste society are erroneous. According to him, the 'traditional Indian society' was not created out of nothing by the British, but that, under them, the institution, flexible originally, became consolidated and, caste hierarchy got more pervasive; the Brahminical interpretation of society which was theoretical earlier now became fully entrenched. C.A. Bayly, *Indian Society and the Making of the British Empire*, Cambridge University Press, Cambridge, 1988.

9. Adrian Mayer, *Land and Society in Malabar*, Oxford University Press, Bombay, 1952, p. 130.
10. Ibid., p. 38.
11. A.R. Narayana Iyer, Letter to The Editor, *Mithavadi*, vol. 3, no. 2, February, 1915, p. 43 As the institution of caste got de-legitimised from the early twentieth century, interestingly, there were stray attempts by individual upper castes to blame others for the horrors of caste. In an article brimming with injured innocence, one Nambudiri in *Mithavadi* lamented about the unfair criticism the naïve, weak, and frightened Nambudiri lot had to take for the practice of untouchability and oppression of the lower castes, when in fact the 'middle castes' [read Nairs] were responsible for the same. Moothiringottu Bhavathrathan Namboodiripad, 'Samudaya Maithri', *Mithavadi*, vol. 4, no. 6, June 1916, p. 46.
12. Mekkunnath Krishnan Nair, 'Sri Laksmana Surendranatha Prabhu: Oru Anusmaranam', *Mathrubhumi*, vol. 22, no. 5, 16 April 1944, p. 3.
13. Adrian Mayer, op. cit., 44.

14. M. Rajavarma Thampan, 'Achaara Navikaranam', *Unni Nambuthiri*, vol. 6, no. 1, 1926, p. 38.
15. Quoted in Murkoth Kunhappa, *Murkoth Kumaran*, Sahitya Pravarthaka Cooperatrive Society Ltd., Kottayam, 1975, p. 149.
16. B. Rajeevan, 'From Caste to Sex: A Study on Sexuality and the Formation of Modern Subject in Kerala' in M.A. Oommen, ed. *Rethinking Development: Kerala's Development Experience*, vol. I, Concept Publishing House, New Delhi, 1999, p. 46.
17. Adrian Mayer, *Land and Society in Malabar*, Oxford University Press, Bombay, 1952, p. 197. Traditionally, even the wearing of ornaments was decided by caste. Lower castes were not meant to wear them while Nambudiri women could not use gold ornaments. Instead, as Dunsterville observed, they used to 'wear silver earrings and many brass armlets' while 'the Nair women wear considerable amounts of jewelery in the way of necklaces, bracelets and ear-ornaments, the last named being large cylinders of gold artistically engraved, inserted in a hole made in the lobe of the ear.' F. Dunsterville, *Illustrated Guide to the Madras Railway*, Higgin Botham and Co., Madras, 1898, p. 50. As for the men, Logan observed that Nambudiri men usually wore only finger-rings, whereas Nairs wore ear-rings. William Logan, *Malabar*, vol. I, Asian Educational Services, New Delhi, 1989 (1st pub. 1887), pp. 134-5.
18. T.K. Gopala Panikkar, *Malabar and its Folk*, G.A. Natesan and Company, Madras, 1901, p. 202.
19. K.P. Kesava Menon, *Kazhinja Kaalam*, The Mathrubhumi Printing and Publishing Company Limited, Calicut, 1986 (1st pub. 1957), pp. 26-7.
20. E.M.S. Namboodiripad, *Atmakatha*, Chintah publishers, Trivandrum, 1985, pp. 128-9.
21. E.M.S. Namboodiripad adds that, as free food was provided at the *Math*, they used to wear the sacred thread again while going there for lunch. Ibid., p. 130.
22. Caroline Osella and Filippo Osella, 'Once Upon a Time in the West: Narrating Modernity in Kerala, South India' in Jaqui Parry and David Arnold, eds. *Life Stories in South India*, Oxford University Press, New Delhi, pp. 46-7.
23. Thampan, op. cit., p. 36.
24. Kunhappa, op. cit., p. 115.
25. Cyriac K. Pullapilly, 'The Izhavas of Kerala and their Historic Struggle for Acceptance in Kerala Society', in Bardwell L. Smith, ed., *Religion and Social Conflict in South Asia*, Brill, Leiden, 1976, p. 37.

26. Mayer, op. cit., p. 43.
27. Ibid., p. 40.
28. E.M.S. Namboodiripad, *Keralam Malayalikalude Mathrubhoomi*, Chintha Publishers, Thiruvanthapuram, 2009 (first published in 1948), p. 250.
29. Gladys Ambat, 'Response', *Government Brennen College Magazine*, vol. VIII, no. 1, December 1939, p. 87.
30. Mangalat Raghavan, 'Poyi Poya Thalamurakal' in *Thalasserry: Sarada Krishnayyar Memorial Fine Arts Society Smaranika*, Chitra DTP Solutions, Tellicherry, 2002, p. 73. In his presidential address on the occasion of the *Sashtipoorthi* of Murkoth Kumaran, Ulloor waxed eloquently of his friendship with the former. According to him, both of them, vassals at the temple of Saraswati, the Goddess of knowledge, enjoyed a special bonding, 'taramaitri', possible due to compatibility of their respective star signs. *Sreeman Murkoth Kumarante Sashtipoorthi Aaghosha Vivaram*, Imperial Printing works, Tellicherry, 1934, p. 2.
31. G. Arunima, 'Glimpses from a Writer's World: O. Chandu Menon, His Contemporaries, and Their Times', *Studies in History*, 20, 2, n.s. (2004), p. 213.
32. Murkoth Kumaran, *Oyarathu Chandu Menon*, Kerala Sahitya Akademi, Thrissur, 1996 (1st pub. 1932), p. 36.
33. Changarakumarath Sankaran, *C. Krishnan*, Sidhartha Book House, Trichur, 1967, p. 20.
34. M.N. Srinivas, *Social Change in Modern India*, Orient Longman, New Delhi, 1977, pp. 94-100.
35. George Mathew, *Communal Road to a Secular Kerala,* Concept Publishing House, New Delhi, 1989. In later years, these caste associations which at one point of time played a revolutionary role were to become quite reactionary under a conservative elite leadership.
36. Reform movements, of course, were carried forward within the respective communities by organizations like the Yogakshema Sabha among the Nambudiris.
37. According to E.M.S. Namboodiripaad, caste system had a progressive role since it enhanced the productive forces through a division of labour. The Nambudiris, he felt, by developing a common language, promoted the cultural unity of the state. And, in practice, while upper caste leaders dominated the party, potential leaders from among the Thiyya community like C.H. Kanaran got ousted from the party at various points in time. Dilip M. Menon, 'Being a Brahmin the Marxist way: E.M.S. Nambudiripad and the Pasts of Kerala', in Daud Ali, ed.

Invoking the Past: The Uses of History in South Asia, Oxford University Press, New Delhi, 1999.

38. Murkoth Srinivasan, 'Apoornamaya Oru Atmakatha', *Mathrubhumi*, vol. 22, no. 16, 2 July 1944, p. 1.
39. K.M. Nair, *Muliyil Krishnan*, Norman Printing Bureau, Calicut, 1932, pp. 72-3.
40. Ibid., p. 73.
41. 'Churyayi Kanaran', unsigned article, *Deepam,* vol. I, no. 7, Kumbham 1930, p. 20.
42. Susan Lewandowsky, *Migration and Ethnicity in Urban India: Kerala Migrants in the City of Madras 1870-1970*, Manohar, New Delhi, 1970, p. 153.
43. Sreedharan Champad, *Circusinte Lokam*, Mathrubhumi Books, Kozhikode, 2008, p. 153.

CHAPTER 5

Negotiating Tradition and Modernity

Pawan Varma in his work on the Indian middle class, while citing Nehru's famous 'Tryst with Destiny' speech in English, claims that the creation of a native elite in its own image was the most spectacular and enduring achievement of British colonialism in India.[1] The triumph of colonialism and its unabashed confidence had given it a rare seductive power, and the members of the Indian middle class from the nineteenth century did not take long in appreciating its civilizational values nor in imitating the lifestyle of those who were sent to govern them. However, it was not a simple process of surrendering fully to the colonizing ideas of the West. While selectively accepting aspects of Western culture, the Indian middle class tried to maintain their distinct identity by possessively clinging on to what they considered the markers of indigenous tradition. On the variations in the attitudes of Bengalis in colonial Bengal towards the West, Sumanta Banerjee observes:

> it was a mixture of admiration and hostility . . . attitudes towards the West ranged from viewing it as a superior civilization that should be emulated, to rejecting it as a 'heathen', materialist culture that threatened the spirituality inclined Orient. . . . In between, stood some who perceived the West as an object of cautious and careful evaluation for adopting selectively from it certain ideas and norms to adapt them to the Bengal context, and move with the times.[2]

This chapter seeks to examine this process in Malabar, the psychological conflicts over identity and belonging for those who desired to 'belong' to two locations at the same time – that of the indigenous as well as the middle class culture of Britain.

Looking to the West

Colonial Malabar, especially from the late nineteenth century witnessed dramatic changes in society and economy. Age-old traditions had to give way to a new order. Pleas were made for making alterations in customs according to changing needs. In one instance, it was pointed out that:

> For various reasons, we have to go to places like Trivandrum and Madras. On such occasions, we have to behave according to the conventions prevalent there and the conveniences available. In Trivandrum, for instance, rules of pollution cannot be maintained like at the *Illam*, and in Madras one cannot possibly take a dip in the pond.[3]

At the turn of the last century, of all the communities, the Nambudiris were probably the most orthodox. Their life at home, especially, was steeped in age-old rituals and superstitions. When, under the influence of the national movement, Indians took to boycott of foreign goods and campaigned for prohibition, a commentator wrote thus about the Nambudiris – 'as they as a community were not as yet influenced by western changes, Nambudiris remain Indians. There is no need for them to consciously pursue ideals like Swadeshi and Prohibition.'[4]

But, even among this community, as the autobiographies of the period reveal, changes would occur from the early twentieth century. The transformation is reflected, for instance, in the way the community responded to Western medicine. Devaki Nilayangodu writes of how in her childhood, the doctor, Krishnayyar, who used to enter the house only after taking bath from the *Illam* pond, would treat only male members of the family. Women would tell their problems from behind doors, and the doctor would prescribe medicines accordingly.

Years later, when along with the times, aesthetics too changed for the Nambudiri women, and keeping long ears grew out of fashion, Devaki, now a married woman, would head for the clinic of the same Krishnayyar to shorten hers.[5]

The changes that were unleashed, consequently, were clearly moulded by colonial modernity. T.K. Gopala Panikkar, one of the earliest natives to write about 'Malabar and its folk' with a modern perspective, observed that 'the social frame, like the human body, is constantly undergoing changes by slow and imperceptible gradations; the nature of these changes being more or less dependent upon the kind of food with which that body is nourished. We are being fed on the strong food of western science and civilisation; and it is no wonder that our life and society are passing through changes resulting from living contact with the west.'[6] Adrian Mayer observed that there existed in Malabar a tolerance and willingness to understand Western institutions. This, according to him, was due to the fact that in contrast to what followed in other parts of India, where the British waged war for years against the local opposition, in Malabar, they first came as traders, a welcome relief after the religious depredations of the Portugese and the warfare of the Dutch, while their second step was again in the line of tolerance after Tipu's excesses.[7]

As the British gained a foothold in the region, and the West became an ideal to be emulated, a lucky few lived out their dream of visiting the 'mother country', a majority of whom went there for higher education. For those who had not yet made the cut, the dream lived on. G. Sankaran Nair wrote 'as days pass on, I long more and more to visit England and other Western countries. I consider a visit to the West is assuredly a part of a liberal education. Would God enable me to fulfill my desires?'[8] Once there, it was the apparent freedom prevalent there that exhilarated many visitors. K.P. Kesava Menon observed,

> the greatest feeling while in London is that we are living in a nation of freedom. Wherever you look, you will find signs of that freedom. The small and the big people can equally use public utilities. You can criticize the administration for its fault without fear through the media. In public places anyone can express his free opinion on whatever issue. In the place where you reside, what else do you need.[9]

Those who had been to the West were to become painfully aware of the differences in hygienic conditions between the two worlds. 'Only after going out and seeing other countries' progress and civilization we become aware of our situation',[10] wrote Kesava Menon in his *Bilathi Visesham*, which recount his experiences in

England. After visiting a market in London, he observed: 'when we see the clean way in which meat and fish are sold here, we are reminded of the dirt and odour of our own place'.[11] And, in colonial Malabar, where, poverty was widespread, and sanitary conditions, like elsewhere in India, primitive, there were often reasons to complain. *Kerala Chandrika* of 13 January 1902 complained of the inconvenience caused to the people by the scavenger's carts being taken up and down the roads at all times of the day.[12] G. Sankaran Nair, while on a train journey, after reluctantly having meals at the Erode railway station, noted in his diary 'the meals were very dirty and even the vessels were not kept clean. The tumblers have not been washed for days together. I am losing faith even in Brahmin hotels.'[13] On another experience during a train journey, he writes: 'I had to chide a passenger for spitting inside the compartment. As a people, I believe we are one of the most insanitary of races. A railway 3rd class wagon is the best evidence of this statement.'[14]

Articles carried in the pages of the magazines of the period castigated the unhygienic conditions prevailing in the country in all walks of life, from 'vegetables sold near drains, of butchers leaving behind meat planks for dogs to come and lick later, of unhygienic servants with infectious diseases, of waiters in hotels with dirt inside their finger nails serving food minutes after scratching their private parts, of people urinating in public places. . . .'[15] Often, demands were made for doctors to examine domestic servants and certify that they are not carrying infectious diseases, and for the Health department to ensure that hygiene was maintained in hotels.[16] The *Kerala Sanchari* of 21 October 1903 advised that sanitary science should be made a compulsory subject at the primary level.[17] Sometimes, concerns for hygiene took extreme forms. The *Kerala Sanchari* of 10 July 1907 demanded that Municipal authorities should prevent people with leprosy, ulcers and other skin diseases of contagious nature from entering the fish market and touching fish.[18] And, all the while, ironically enough, the myth of Malayali cleanliness was being invented at the expense of a dirty other, who, more often than not, happened to be the unfortunate Tamilian neighbour, who allegedly was prone 'not to take regular baths nor wash his clothes!'[19]

The colonizers had deplored the absence of a citizen-culture on the part of the natives, of the absence of a civic life and 'public interest among them, of the disorder of the streets, and of the lack of hygiene in the open spaces'. But this discourse on hygiene – or lack of it – did not remain confined to the colonizers. It was not long before the Westernized natives imbibed such prejudices from their colonial masters. As Dipesh Chakravarty argues, this 'language of modernity, of civic consciousness and public health, of even certain ideas of beauty related to the management of public space and interests, an order of aesthetics from which the ideals of public health and hygiene cannot be separated . . . is the language of modern governments, both colonial and postcolonial, and for that reason it is the language of not only of imperialist officials but of modern nationalists as well.'[20]

The irony was that, historically, Indians were more hygienic than their British counterparts. For instance, in India, even in the pre-colonial times, bathing using traditional cleansing agents existed, while in England, up to the eighteenth century, bathing was very rare. Even then, the Indian elites fell under the sway of the colonial myth that Indians were dirty, sweaty and smelly. Once, during the late colonial period, industrially manufactured soaps became available, the Western educated Indians trying to overcome this 'inadequacy' took to them with a passion. As Harminder Kaur observes, the regard for Western progress, in particular, towards science and technology, and the subsequent desire to prove Indian adequacy, got reflected in the production and consumption of cosmetics and grooming products in the early twentieth century.[21]

The advertisements of the period provide ample evidence to how modern soaps were replacing the more traditional cleansing agents. A passage from the memoirs of P.K.S. Kutty, the cartoonist, reveals the changes:

> The most common medium used to clean one's body was a fine powder made from the bark of a tree. This was called vaka. . . . But civilization was already creeping upon us. My father was selling soap which was imported from England. . . . The soaps available were Pears and Vinolia White Rose for bathing and Sunlight for washing clothes. . . . Many years later, when the Lux soap hit the market, it was a sensation. The jasmine perfume of that soap used to pervade the whole atmosphere round the tank for hours.

My mother opted for soap before all others in our locality. Soaps drove the vaka out of the market. [22]

It was encounters like these with products like soaps that, in many cases, represent the first engagement the natives had with modernity.

Those who had the opportunity to visit England had been impressed by the material and scientific progress achieved there, and the rational spirit which guided its people. They felt that India could achieve progress only if its people were able to give up on their superstitious beliefs. This explains the context in which, for instance, a sustained critique was leveled against astrology, and its pretensions to being a 'science'. In the novel *Storm and Sunshine*, the hero's mother opposes the marriage of her son to Madhavi on astrological grounds once she comes to know that the latter had a bad star sign which would lead to the ruin of her husband if she married. Then, Sekhara Warrier, an older relative with some English education, through a scathing critique on astrology, put things in perspective:

> How many are the existing nations of the earth other than ourselves who do not care a farthing for astrological predictions. . . . It is now practiced as a science, a position which it has no shadow of a right to be elevated to. . . . The predictions of astrologers will, if minutely scrutinized, necessarily contain ambiguous or contradictory words that are capable of two exactly different interpretations, alike to the famous replies of the old Greek Oracles of Delphi. . . . If we compare the different nations of the earth, how their rise and progress are regulated and marked, we will find that those that are tied down by the pernicious influences of hoary past are immensely low in the scale of progress; while those that have been amenable to the healthy influences of change and progress have risen considerably high and are at this day occupying the forefront amongst the nations of earth.[23]

Western education gave a body blow to the traditional world view. Autobiographies of E.M.S. Namboodiripad[24] and C. Sankaran Nair reveal how belief in the supernatural erodes fully by the time one's education is complete. To quote from the autobiography of the latter:

> We had our own Kuladevata [household deity]. . . . There were festivals held in honour of the goddess and on such occasions there was a large

pile of burning timber stacked. After the ceremony the young men of the village, myself included, used, after a dip in the tank, to walk through the fire and scatter the burning wood about. Not one of us was ever hurt. After I was grown up, I could not even approach such a burning fire. My faith had gone.[25]

There was the growing belief that progress had been achieved by the English as a nation by adhering to certain values. Thus, in the middle-class discourses in Malabar during this period, there was the valorization of such values as punctuality, thrift, hardwork, etc. With the growth of cities and, associated with it, factories and various offices, the value of time was realized. Life was no longer as relaxed and casual as it used to be in the past. The need for punctuality to make the best use of time was understood. K.P. Kesava Menon, educated in England, best exemplified this. His grandson observes:

What struck me most in his ways is the absolute punctuality that he maintains in all his appointments and regular routines. Whether it is the breakfast walk or the pre-breakfast session of writing that he does, or the breakfast and lunch times, afternoon naps, attending public meetings or trips to other parts of Kerala, he does all these on the specific hours of the clock.[26]

But, a majority of the population, slowly coming out of the old order, took time to adjust to the new requirements.[27] As one sarcastically put it, 'Punctuality . . . is a plant which attained full growth in Western countries at a very early time, but in our own country, or rather, in our hemisphere, its germinative power has always been rather low. There has therefore come into existence here a new stunted variety called Indian punctuality.'[28] *Kerala Chandrika* of 14 September 1900, reports of officials including *tahsildars* and other revenue department officials in Malabar coming to their offices very late, some turning up only at 2'o clock, causing inconvenience not only to their subordinates but also to those who visited from distant places.[29]

Corruption and sycophancy, which vitiate Indian public life to this day, had their silent adherents as well as vocal critics even in those days. According to a section of the educated Indians, the English were free of these vices. Kesava Menon, for instance, felt that 'inspite of the traditions of Harishchandra and Sri Rama, in real life, we are not very honest. . . . The British, on the other hand, do not relate honesty to religion, but to every day practical social life to make business social interaction better.'[30] 'Not for them' he went on to observe, 'the habit of "oiling" their superiors in their chambers, and then, coming out of it, making empty boasts'.[31]

Even as the rat-race among the middle classes in a colonial mileu which offered very few career opportunities to them was ridiculed, it was, nevertheless, realized that one had to be ambitious in order to succeed. Write-ups on successful men, and manuals on how to succeed in life were common in the magazines of the period. It was advised that 'legitimate ambition is what we should all aim at. To rest content is to be unambitious . . . [which] proves to be one of a low mental caliber and effeminate character. Vaulting ambition is such that which pricks the sides of our intent, enlivens our spirits, and puts on our mettle.'[32] Among the middle classes, many examples are thrown up of those who excelled in more than one walk of life. C. Krishnan, a lawyer ended up being a publisher and prominent businessman. Appu Nedungadi, a pioneering Malayalam novelist, owned one of the earliest indigenously owned banks in the region. M. Kumaran was a teacher as well as a literary figure. So too Sanjayan, while O. Chandu Menon acquired lasting fame with his literary work, combining an illustrious career in the judiciary. When this was the model, laziness became a vice which had to be got rid off. While in England, M.A. Candeth anxiously wrote in his diary of how his dreamy nature was making him prone to laziness:

> having no companion and no one to talk to, my imagination carries me away. This coupled with Gibbon makes me indulge in all sorts of fancies. I think it is a very bad habit. It may grow upon me, and make me a dreamer. Already, it takes me away from real work. Makes me idle, lazy, indolent, etc. It is the greatest of all evils to which a young man can fall prey to.[33]

While laziness had to be got rid off, self-reliance, which traditional India with its joint family and pampering of children prevented from developing was projected as something to be aspired. To quote M.A. Candeth again: 'I now realize the evil of being brought up like a baby at home. It creates shyness, nervousness, dependency on others and a very great lack of self-confidence.'[34]

Up to the end of the nineteenth century, at a general level, individualism and individuality were marked by their absence in the country. Instead one's destiny was more or less controlled by the institutions of family, caste, and community. The concept of self was to develop during the late colonial period.

The growing feeling was that one should try to stand on one's own feet. Self-made men became the role models. In the novel *Premabandham,* Krishnanunni, the son of Kesava Menon's *Karyasthan*, falls in love with Devakikutty, Kesava Menon's niece. Her father tells him to make Rs. 5,000 within one year, after which he would consider his proposal hoping he would not be able to do so. A kindly Ammukutty, Devakikutty's mother who could understand the young couple's agony, offers the amount, but he declines, stressing the need to stand on one's own feet, and earn one's own money. He goes to Madras, and with great difficulty earns the amount while working as a coolie.[35] Similarly, living off one's inheritance was looked down upon. In its attempt to contest the cultural, economic and political significance of the feudal lords, the middle class stressed the importance of individual achievement over birth. It tried to distinguish itself from the decadent feudal classes by emphasizing the desirability of thrift and industry over conspicuous consumption and idleness. Nambudiris who had been a privileged group in the past and were not known for their hard work, but had instead lived off their inherited property were perhaps the last to adopt these values. Critiques from the younger generation of the community in the reformist journals about such a lifestyle were frequent. The reformers among the Nambudiris criticized those among the older generation in the community who still lived in the past and remained unmindful of the importance of work. It was pointed out that

> many assume that as work is meant to earn money, who does not need the latter can do without the former. They then go on to enjoy the wealth created by their ancestors. . . . In truth, the pleasure enjoyed by them is akin to the one who lies down in the night but cannot sleep. . . . With one's own earnings, people should take care of their family. Public opinion has changed. If we do not change our ways, we shall end up licking the boots of other communities.[36]

Being middle class, thus, meant, apart from other things, taking responsibility for one's self, one's family and the community. The system of *Mallikhana*, whereby ex-chieftains were given state pensions was bitterly criticized:

> It is a criminal waste to continue the payment of lakhs of rupees in the shape of political pensions to certain idlers who have no moral right to this public charity. It is one of the many anomalies of Malabar that it is exceptionally rich in political pensioners on whose account the people are fleeced to the extent of three lakhs or more year after year; that is, 10 per cent of the land revenue of Malabar is spent on the maintenance of an anthropological Museum of Rajas. . . . No other community would feed this blood sucking parasite on its body politic.[37]

The Call of Tradition

According to Sanjay Joshi, modernity was a contradictory conception. It brought with it new anxieties about self, health, sexuality, family, work and social order; it was fractured by 'traditional' values and by economic realities.[38] As Western culture held sway, and more and more people came under its sway, it gave rise to discontent amongst those who felt that the indigenous tradition was being irrevocably damaged. It was pointed out that 'an impoverishment of the mind and the spirit, far worse than any material poverty, has overtaken us'.[39] The constant reminder was that even if we have to cooperate with the West as an alien power is now ruling us, it should not be at the expense of 'disrespecting our age-old national character, disciplined way of life and glorious tradition'.[40] In the pages of the several magazines that mushroomed during this period, Western culture was frequently referred to as being selfish and vulgarly materialist, which often led to undesirable consequences. In spite of enjoying material comforts, it was pointed out that people in the West were generally unhappy. Pointing to the many killings, suicides and accidental deaths which occur in London on a regular basis, K.P. Kesava Menon observed that 'along with the benefits of modern civilization, one has to bear in mind its flaws as well'.[41]

For some like Chandu Menon, who had become familiar with the best of Western literature and science through the medium of

English, this language provided a beacon of hope for the natives. As P.K. Balakrishnan has shown, in Chandu Menon's two novels, *Indulekha* and *Sarada*, not a single character who knows English is portrayed in a bad light while the Nambudiris, who turned their back on English education, are generally ridiculed.[42] 'Perhaps', Balakrishnan observes, 'Chandu Menon links their lack of humanism due to the distance they kept from the English language!'[43]

But not everyone shared his faith in the English system of education. Ramankutty Menon's satirical novel *Parangodi Parinayam*, which appeared in 1892 and had good sales, upholds values diametrically opposite to those of *Indulekha*, and represents the conservative reaction to English education and renaissance.[44] The anglicized heroine Parangodi likes tea and reads *London Times*, and is not averse to courting before marriage. In a chapter which echoes/parodies the famous chapter in *Indulekha* where Madhavan dwells on religion and politics, among other things, Panghasha Menon, who stands by tradition, critiques those who blindly imitate the West as hollow and superficial. In the end, the anglicized hero and heroine, totally alienated from the community, end up unmarried. Unlike, *Indulekha*, there is no happy ending here.[45]

There were people too who, during this time, outwardly endorsed reforms, but not entirely with conviction, and got lampooned in the literature of the times like Kesava Menon was in *Premabandham*. A lawyer in his thirties who had served in Madras, Menon was depicted as a hypocrite in the novel patronizing the press and government servants, to ensure his image as a reformer while leading a traditional life in private.[46]

In *Indulekha*, the English language becomes a sign of terror for those deprived of it.[47] When Madhavan rebels against the *Karanavan* in the very first scene of the novel, both the latter and Madhavan's uncle belonging to the earlier generation are taken aback and cites Madhavan's English education as a source for his attitude. On another occasion when Indulekha repulses his advances, Surya Namboodiripad assumes that English education has killed her feminine qualities, and goes on to marry Indulekha's cousin Kalyanikutty after ensuring that she is not English educated!

Like the Bengali satirist of colonial Bengal, who targeted

the mimic men or surrogate baboos, we find in Malabar too, his Malayali counterpart taking to task those who had abjectly surrendered to the West. Vengayil Kunhiraman Nayanar writes of how some people even smile in English which is different from the indigenous version![48] Some lamented the decline of the Malayalam language as people took to the learning of the English language in the process of which, one became proficient neither in English nor Malayalam. It was felt that those who got government jobs had a very shallow knowledge of the English language. Kesari gives the example of a recently appointed magistrate who, not knowing the English language used to make a model of earlier judgements in that language, memorize it, and changing the date and names, pass judgements accordingly![49] As Gauri Vishwanathan puts it in the pan-Indian context, 'English education came to be criticized for its imitativeness and superficiality and for having produced an uprooted elite who were at once apostates to their own national tradition and imperfect imitators of the west.'[50]

Under the impact of colonial modernity, the region witnessed sartorial changes. In the wake of a recently acquired sexualized subjectivity, with its notions of modesty and nudity, partly helped by the gendered divisions deployed in schools and colleges run by the missionaries and the government, an anglicized middle class took to a European style of dress as is indicated in the photos and fiction of the period. For many, Western dress was regarded as symbols of Europeanization and of the economic efficiency and power that were supposed to result there from. Sartorial changes, however, did not remain uncontested. Sections of the same middle class expressed the view that there cannot be just one modernity irrespective of geography, time, environment, and social conditions. It was pointed out how our climate requires us to wear clothes which allow free flow of air and sunlight. In a sense, the indigenous response to the onslaught of colonial modernity can be located within the limits and framework set by colonial discourse. Bernard Cohn has shown how in the colonial discourse a distinction was made between the European body and its Indian counterpart, and the need for the former to have a different set of clothes to tackle the harsh Indian weather.[51]

Some influential sections in Malabar used more or less fully Western dress except for the traditional headgear and the *mundu* in public. One example would be Murkoth Kumaran who, according to his biographer, used golden specs, English twill shirt, black tie, coat, walking stick, shoes and a headgear.[52] Mayer describes the compromise the Malayali male made with regard to dress thus, 'the *mundu* is retained and a western shirt worn over it . . . trousers are certainly not advantageous in the Malabar climate.'[53] There were some like Sanjayan, who, though he used to talk only in English to students while in class and the staffroom, did not like wearing English dress. But then, it was compulsory to wear suit, tie and boots to Malabar Christian College. So, as a kind of compromise, he used to come to college in a suit, but once inside the class room, used to take it off![54] P.K.S. Kutty, in his memoirs, recounts how incongruous it looked when some of his teachers at Malabar Christian College in the 1930s amalgamated the Western attire with the regional, '*mundu* and jacket, and sandalwood paste/ash on the forehead along with ties!'[55] Of such people, the vernacular press was often acerbic in its criticism. One commentator wrote of how 'there is no shortage of vulgar attire we have made by mixing two or three parts of European dress with ours. Up to the neck it is like a European; overhead like a native . . . [as a result] most of our reformers look like devils.'[56] In *Storm and Sunshine*, the author sarcastically talks of 'those born with silver spoons in their mouths, dressed in flannel shirts, and native fashioned caps, some chewing betel, some sending off whiffs from cigars and cigarettes'.[57] It is not that those who wore Western attire always felt comfortable in it. Even a stay in England did not help, in some cases, in getting rid of the unease one felt in a new attire. M.A. Candeth, during his stay in England, once entered in his diary that 'we look queer in this European dress. We lose all our charm in western dress'.[58]

The wasteful spending on clothes and fashion was denounced. Here, women assumed to be lavish in their spending for non-productive purposes, were the main target in cartoons and advertisements of the time.[59] Fashion was identified with an enslavement to Western goods and norms, selfishness, sexual promiscuity, and the break-up of the joint family.[60]

The 1920s and 1930s were marked by an economic slump. The middle class, consequently went through a crisis. On the one hand, they needed to maintain a certain lifestyle to remain 'middle class', but at the same time, avoid unnecessary expenditure to avoid complete penury. Prashant Kidambi has shown how in western India during this period, manuals and books advised the middle classes to lead a simple lifestyle abjuring all forms of wanton or wasteful expenditure in order to be self-reliant, happy and contented.[61]

At a time when cake and jam as well as the use of fork and knife had become common,[62] a critique was also made against Western food habits, which was alleged to have destroyed our health. Instead of learning from what is best in the Western civilization, it was pointed out that we are merely imitating their worst aspects, which will 'result in an increase in expenses and decline in the lifespan'.[63] Readers were often warned against the intake of tea and coffee after the British as it could lead to health problems ranging from lack of appetite to heart-seizures as our hot climate was not conducive for their intake.[64] It was lamented that in a poor country like ours 'out of the little money we make, three-fourth of it goes for expenses leading to health problems'.[65] The importance of a proper and timely diet in the maintenance of physical and mental health was recognized. At the time of his *Sashtipoorthi* (sixtieth birthday) celebrations, in his reply speech, Murkoth Kumaran stated that eating moderately, and only when he was hungry was the sole reason for his healthy and still youthful looks.[66] He also made it clear, on this occasion, that if the pangs of hunger got to him while away from home, he would approach his nearest friend's house to satisfy it instead of going to a restaurant.[67]

Alcohol was considered a direct by-product of Western culture. Abolitionism or a critique of alcoholism became a byword in middle-class discourse during this period. In an editorial in *Mithavadi*, C. Krishnan wrote 'alcohol gives nothing but harm to society. Three-fourths of the miseries in the world are caused by alcohol. . . . Alcohol gives courage to murderers; causes breakdown of families, results in intestinal problems, heart diseases, etc. leading to untimely death.'[68] In April 1928, during his presidential address during the second anniversary of Valappat Sree Narayana Guru Smaraka Samaj, he went further and said that 'there is no difference between an animal and an alcoholic'.[69] Several articles came up in the magazines of the period denouncing the consumption of alcohol, and proposing ways to get rid of it. *Kerala Patrika* of 11 May 1889 stated that 'with a view to discourage intemperance as much as possible, the number of liquor shops should be reduced to four or five in each taluk, selling of liquor on credit should be punished, and increased duty should be levied on foreign liquors imported'.[70] But others argued that measures including the hike in the price of alcohol would not be a solution, and, instead, wanted a total ban on it, 'If price increases, the alcoholic would indulge in dacoity; if, on the other hand, it was decreased, the whole family would starve as the father would spend all available money on it. Due to the drinking problem, the poor is the most affected. The only solution is to ensure alcohol is not available.'[71] The link between alcoholism and poverty was noted by some. For instance, it was observed that 'any remedy that does not go to the root of the evil must assuredly meet with failure. The raising of the price of alcohol may fatten the brewer and enhance the public revenue but can never promote the cause of temperance. It must be the duty of the reformer, then, to attack the motives for intemperance, to attack poverty, care and sorrow. Lectures and periodicals are good in their own way; but when addressed to a starving man, they are empty mockeries '. . . If all the money raised for conference and temperance literature be spent in giving the starving wretches a hearty meal, the genuineness of our sympathy might be appreciated. . . . Remove poverty, then of its pangs and sorrow of its stings and you have solved the problem of drink.'[72]

For some amongst the middle class, inspite of conceding to the liberating aspects of Western culture, a few of its features were plainly terrifying, for instance, the invasive nature of imperial medicine. In one of his pieces, Sanjayan, in his inimitable style, admits how he, wary of typhoid vaccination, tried to avoid it, but finally was forced to undergo it, giving details of his fears beforehand and the consequences thereafter.[73] While talking of his childhood in a village, E.M.S Namboodiripad mentions the police and the vaccinators as representatives of the feared colonial power. 'While playing excitedly', he recalls, 'if a policeman or vaccinator comes, we used go into hiding. And, if anyone came in suit, assuming he was a vaccinator, we used to run away in fear.'[74] Western medicine, while making advances in the region from the late nineteenth century, did invite the wrath of the natives. The *Kerala Patrika* of 5 April 1912, while defending the continued existence of the Ayurvedic and Unani practitioners, which were still popular among the natives, stressed the desirability of registering medical practitioners in the European system and the requirement to possess license before practising because compounders and ward boys dabbling in medicine were causing much harm and mischief among patients.[75] There were calls to revive Kerala's traditional Ayurvedic medicine, which was believed to suit better the constitution of the natives. P.S. Variar, who started the Kottakkal Arya Vaidya Sala in 1902, exemplified this spirit best. In an issue of *Dhanwantari*, the fortnightly published from Kottakkal, he distinguished between the bodies of the European and the Indian, and consequently the different medical systems required for both:

> In Europe warmth is considered an indicator of happiness, as evident from the use of words 'warm reception'. In contrast, we use the word *santapam* (heat) for sorrow. . . . The climate being cold, Europeans feel happy with a little warmth. We, on the other hand, living in a tropical region are fond of cold. If any medicine to generate heat in the body is to be administered to Europeans, it has to be quite strong. Their medicines prepared to suit the body of Europe are too hot for us. For those living in tropical countries, an important quality of medicine is the ability of cooling the system . . . their medicines are effective for their diseases but not suitable for the conditions of our body.[76]

It was pointed out that government's encouragement extended to Allopathy through training institutes to train potential medical practitioners, hospitals and dispensaries, and the commercial techniques developed by Western medicine helped it to advance, while Ayurvedic medicine, which was given step-motherly treatment, declined.[77]

Modernity of Tradition

The new middle class, a product of colonial modernity, in its attempts to maintain its roots, clung on to tradition. A framework that juxtaposes tradition *versus* modernity as binaries is no longer in vogue. Thus, in Malabar too, an approach which places a generation of educated Malayalis steeped in Western values going all out against the archaic institutions does not stand scrutiny. The contraries present in the votaries of tradition and modernity were not absolute, nor essentially oppositional, instead there were, often, overlapping elements of both in each other. Amongst the middle classes, there were many who lamented the 'abject surrender' to the West. Even those who glorified the West otherwise, in some cases, were critical of blindly imitating it. This ambiguity, as argued by Joshi in the case of colonial Lucknow, could be seen as a result of the 'fractured modernity' which marks the colonial experience as far as India was concerned.[78] This explains the simultaneous articulations of what appears to be contradictory positions on political, social and cultural issues.

Nowhere is this ambiguity more in evidence than in the divergent positions taken by Chandu Menon with regard to changes in marriage laws in Malabar. Menon, who in his novels clearly demonstrated his preference for monogamous marriages and nuclear families, exhibited a far more conservative approach with regard to the Malabar Marriage Bill. When under some pressure from sections in Malabar, the colonial regime made efforts to legalize the *sambandham* form of marriage, Menon spoke against the proposed bill of Sri C. Sanakran Nair on the ground that a registered marriage system did not recognize caste restrictions. He expressed his horror at an 'appalling' scenario where 'an *anandaravan* (nephew) brings a pariah wife' following which 'the whole of the members of the *tarawad* if they wish to keep up their caste and social status will have to leave their *tarawad* house and live elsewhere'.[79] Chandu Menon here represents the colonial middle-class anxiety to catch up with the West, to become modern, but not at the expense of erasing their identity in the process. Drawing a distinction between the Orient and the Occident he argued against the universalization of values:

It is always difficult to defend or justify the social and religious customs of Oriental nations according to the European notion of morality and theology . . . each nation values its own custom in respect of its marriage and other social and religious institutions independently of what other people think of them and to a certain extent each nation has got its own code of morality in respect of such institutions.[80]

Similarly, Govindan, the hero in *The Wound of Spring*, tries to modernize the *tarawad* in order to save it from extinction.[81]

According to Partha Chatterjee, 'the discourse of reason was not unequivocally liberating [for the colonized middle class] . . . [Instead, the colonizer's] condemnation of indigenous culture as the storehouse of unreason made it oppressive'.[82] There were many among the new middle classes who, while imbibing what the modern West had to offer, remained faithful to their tradition. Though there were the odd atheists, religious attitude was, as yet, not regarded as a binary to scientific thought. The *Gurukulam* published by the teachers of the Nettur Training School was filled with articles on science and reason, but were interlaced with pieces on puranic themes, and, significantly, on the front page it was stated that 'devotion to God marks the beginning of knowledge'. In the eighteenth chapter of *Indulekha,* during a debate on religion, Madhavan, a product of modern education takes a position which favours religion minus its superstitions, an attitude representative of the new middle class.[83] In a long discussion on the practical relevance of religion, Murkoth Kumaran observes:

An individual may decide whether he will believe in God or not. But this prerogative does not apply to society as a whole. When crimes and injustices occur in societies where the majority of people believe in God, what would happen to societies where God does not exist. . . . In educationally backward communities, if faith in God, which help inculcate values, disappear will their members be any different from animals?[84]

The changing family laws, and the decline of the *Tarawad* system, brought in their wake, discontent even in unexpected quarters. Krishna Menon, who was educated in England as well as spent most of his adult life prior to independence there, had been keeping in touch with his family in Malabar. As his niece recounts in his biography, he had a bitter conflict with her non-Malayali father – 'who thought the matriarchal system a bit of a joke at its best, or downright unreasonable at its worst' – when the latter prevented him from exercising his rights over the family as a *karanavan* (male head of the household).[85]

Those who made it during the colonial period were not those who rejected the Western culture in its entirety or those who blindly accepted it in toto. Instead, what an influential and ultimately successful section did was a selective appropriation of the ideas of the West, while, at the same time, rejecting what was considered inappropriate. The ideal projected was somebody like the hero and the heroine of *Indulekha* – modern educated but rooted in their moorings, where there is a neat blending of indigenous and Western values. As Kainikkara M. Kumara Pillai writes:

> through his hero and heroine he [O. Chandu Menon] presents a healthy and inspiring ideal to the new generation, a harmonious synthesis of all that is best in the East and the West. They have deep reverence for the ancient heritage, but do not hesitate to strip of its sanctified trappings of outmoded customs and hoary superstitions. They warmly welcome the social refinements and the robust rationalism of the West, but are not prepared to ape its outlandish ways.[86]

In real life, there are several examples of individuals who combined features of the East and the West. Krishna Menon, who, as we saw above, held on to illusions of the powers of the *karanavan* even while living in England at a time when the institution was dying out, in a letter to his sister in 1926, wrote about what he thought would be an ideal education for her daughters: 'I would like to see them getting a good grounding in Sanskrit in the old way and to learn lots of music of the best type and be able to play as many instruments as they can and ultimately to be able to be proficient in the scientific side also. I would also like it if they have the talent, to learn English music and Eurythmics.'[87]

That tradition and modernity were not dichotomous, and even in the apparently most modern of men, elements of tradition persisted is best exemplified by the life of Subrahmanyam Thirumunpu. One of the leading lights of the early communist movement in the state, he was seen as a radical, and following the party adopting the Calcutta thesis, had even spent time underground. After coming out of prison, however, he turned spiritual and spent the rest of his life writing books on religion. His wife, however, in her autobiography writes that he had all along been spiritual, offering prayers every morning, and as a child, infact, had seriously considered becoming a sanyasi.[88]

It was not just a case of individuals. Even entrepreneurial enterprises which survived the colonial era had to combine in their ethos the spirit of both the worlds. None epitomized this spirit better than the Kottakkal Arya Vaidya Sala which adopted modern Western methods to survive in an increasingly capitalist ethos even while upholding its traditional values and beliefs.[89] And, its founder, P.S. Variar, according to his biographer, 'was a strong link who joined the old generation with modern reforms, leading his life by accepting the good in both the new as well as the old.'[90]

In summing up, it can be said that throughout the British period, a not too insignificant number of natives blindly imitated Western culture including its defining attire as well as its dietary habits. At the same time, there were many who completely rejected anything and everything Western. Having said that, however, it should be borne in mind that the two groups were not always binaries, and that there were the occasional overlapping, the not too infrequent sharing of traits. Ultimately, it was an educated elite who, while remaining loyal to some of the basic tenets of the traditional culture, selectively adopted features of Western culture who succeeded in the colonial mileu.

NOTES

1. Pavan K. Varma, *The Great Indian Middle Class*, Penguin Books, New Delhi, 1998, pp. 1-2.
2. Sumanta Banerjee, 'The West Turned "Upside Down" in a Bengali Satire', in C. Vijayasree, ed., *Writing the West: Representations from Indian Languages*, Sahitya Akademi, New Delhi, 2004, pp. 24-5.
3. C.S. Subramanya Potti, 'Aachara Parishkarathinte Aavishyakatha-3', *Aatmaposhini*, vol. 6, no. 9, 1916, p. 265.

4. C. Kunhirama Menon, Cheruppakarude Utharavadittam, *Unni Nambuthiri*, vol. 3, no. 4, 1097.
5. Devaki Nilayangodu, *Kaalappakarchakal*, Mathrubhumi Books, Kozhikode, 2008, pp. 120-1.
6. T.K. Gopala Panikkar, *Malabar and its Folk*, G.A. Natesan and Company, Madras, 1901, p. vi.
7. Adrian Mayer, *Land and Society in Malabar*, Oxford University Press, Bombay, 1952, p. 25. Clearly, the author ignores the Pazhassi rebellion, and the Mappila uprisings which took place in Colonial Malabar.
8. Diary of G. Sankaran Nair, dated 10 November 1926.
9. K.P. Kesava Menon, *Bilathi Visesham*, Mathrubhumi Books, Kozhikode, 2007 (1st pub. 1916), p. 66. The odd exceptions, of course, were there. After marvelling at the natural beauty of Italy and the artistic excellence of France, C.T. Philip, Chemistry lecturer at Brennen College, who went to England for higher studies, wrote 'London was to most of us a great disappointment. Its buildings look grim and somber in keeping with the grave and stern people that walk its streets.' C.T. Philip, 'My Journey to England', *Government Brennen College Magazine*, vol. VIII, no. 1, December 1939, p. 6.
10. Menon, op. cit., p. 83.
11. Ibid., p. 30.
12. *Kerala Chandrika*, 13 January 1902 in NNPR for the week ending 18 January 1902, pp. 30-1.
13. Diary of G. Sankaran Nair, dated 21 June 1926.
14. Ibid., dated 27 June 1922.
15. M. Ananthan, 'Shuchithva bodham', *Mathrubhumi*, vol. 20, no. 30, 11 October 1942, p. 11.
16. Ibid., p. 11.
17. *Kerala Sanchari*, 21 October 1903, in NNPR for the week ending 24 October 1903, p. 392.
18. *Kerala Sanchari*, 10 July 1907 in NNPR for the week ending 18 July 1907, p. 221.
19. Vidvan P. R. Variar, 'Malayaliyum Tamizhanum', *Mathrubhumi*, vol. 22, no. 26, 10 September 1944, p. 4.
20. Dipesh Chakrabarty, 'Open Space/Public Place: Garbage, Modernity and India', *South Asia*, vol. XIV, no. 1 (1991), p. 16.
21. Harminder Kaur, 'Of Soaps and Scents: Corporeal Cleanliness in Urban Colonial India', in Douglas E. Haynes et al., eds., *Towards a History of Consumption in South Asia*, Oxford University Press, New Delhi, 2010, p. 254.

22. P.K.S. Kutty, *Years of Laughter: Reminiscences of a Cartoonist*, Thema, Kolkata, 2009, p. 28.
23. T.K. Gopala Panikkar, *Storm and Sunshine: A Novel Illustrative of Malayalee Domestic Life*, The Norman Printing Bureau, Calicut, 1916, pp. 99-103.
24. E.M.S. Namboodiripad who begins his autobiography with a chapter on 'Gods and Demons' had, by his youth, become an ardent devotee of historical materialism. E.M.S. Namboodiripad, *Atmakatha*, Chintah Publishers, Trivandrum, 1985.
25. C. Sankaran Nair, *Autobiography of Chettur Sankaran Nair*, Chettur Sankaran Nair Foundation, Ottapalam, 1998 (1st pub. 1966), p. 1.
26. Venu Menon, 'My Grandfather', in K.P.S. Menon, ed., *Kesava Menon 90*, K.P. Kesava Menon 90th Birthday Celebration Committee, Calicut, 1977, p. 207.
27. According to Sumit Sarkar, transition to capitalism in the West took place at a leisured pace, and the Europeans could internalize, over time, the work-ethic required for the successful functioning of capitalism. While in India, under colonial conditions, an alienated middle class, especially those in clerical posts, found it difficult to adjust to the sudden and harsh conditions of colonial modernity including its clock-time, impersonal cash-nexus and an insensitive authority. Sumit Sarkar, 'Renaissance and Kaliyuga: Time, Myth and History in Colonial Bengal', in *Writing Social History*, Oxford University Press, New Delhi, 2006, p. 190.
28. P. Indira, 'My Punctuality', *The Zamorin's College Magazine*, vol. XIX, no. 1, August 1947, p. 52.
29. *Kerala Chandrika,* 14 September 1900 in NNPR for the week ending 30 September 1900, p. 270.
30. K.P. Kesava, op. cit., p. 117.
31. Ibid., p. 90.
32. V.M.M.N, 'Ambition', *The Zamorin's College Magazine*, vol. 1, no. 1, August 1912, p. 22.
33. Diary of M.A. Candeth, dated 05-09-1907.
34. Ibid., dated 29-05-1907.
35. Variath Balakrishna Menon, *Premabandham*, Durgalaya Press, Chittur, Cochin, 1917. But it was all to no avail. By the time he came back, his lover had been already married off, and both meet with untimely death. Ibid., pp. 47-8.
36. K. Sankaran Namboodiripad, 'Yuvajanangalum Pravarthiyum', *Unni Nambudiri*, vol. 8, no. 7, 1927, pp. 393-400.

37. *Mithavadi*, 25 September 1922 in NNPR for the week ending 28 October 1922, p. 1307.
38. Sanjay Joshi, *Fractured Modernity: Making of a Middle Class in Colonial North India*, New Delhi, Oxford University Press, 2001.
39. Pattathil Padmanabha Menon, 'Athunikarude Anashasyangalayala Chila Anukaranangal', *Kairali*, vol. 3, nos. 7-8, Chingam, 1918, p. 14.
40. R. Iswara Pillai,'Nammude Parishkaram', *Gurunathan*, vol. 6, no. 11, 1927, p. 12.
41. Kesava Menon, op. cit., p. 31.
42. P.K. Balakrishnan, *Chandu Menon: Oru Padanam*, Sahitya Pravarthaka Cooperative Society, Kottayam, 1957, p. 71.
43. Ibid., p. 70.
44. Kizhekkepattu Ramankutty Menon, *Parangodi Parinayam* (1st pub. 1892), in George Irumbayam, ed., *Naalu Novelukal*, Kerala Sahitya Akademi, Trichur, 1985.
45. Ibid.
46. Variath Balakrishna Menon, op. cit.
47. K.M. Narendran, 'Mrigabalikal Vijayolsavangal', *Mathrubhumi Weekly*, 25-31 October 1998, p. 32.
48. Kesari Vengayil Kunhiraman Nayanar, 'Prachina Acharopacharangalum Sthanamanangalum Mattum Mattum', in *Prabhadangalum, Kathakalum Mattum*, (Compilation of earlier articles he published in *Kerala Chandrika, Kerala Patrika*, etc.), Bharatavilasam Press, Trichur, 1956, p. 117. M.P. Sivadasa Menon observed how certain Malayalis refused to keep indigenous dogs as pets and went for foreign ones like spaniels and terriers when the former would have worked out cheaper and more effective. M.P. Sivadasa Menon, *Malabarile Sikkaru*, DC Books, Kottayam, 2002 (1st pub. 1959), p. 23.
49. Kesari Vengayil Kunhiraman Nayanar, 'Swabhasha', in op. cit., p. 223.
50. Gauri Vishwanathan, *Masks of Conquest: Literary Study and British Rule in India*, Faber and Faber, London, 1990, p. 159.
51. Bernard Cohn, *Colonialism and its Forms of Knowledge*, Oxford University Press, New Delhi, 1997, pp. 106-62.
52. Murkoth Kunhappa, *Murkoth Kumaran*, Sahitya Pravarthaka Cooperative Society Ltd., Kottayam, 1975, pp. 125-6.
53. Adrian Mayer, op. cit., pp. 110-11. Wearing trousers was not yet very common even in the 1940s. P.K.S. Kutty remembers that upto independence, no one, except the government servants and professionals like doctors and lawyers, went about in trousers in Ottapalam. P.K.S. Kutty, op. cit., p. 44.

54. Prabhakaran Pazhassi, *Sanjayan: Kalathinte Manasaakshi*, Department of Cultural Publications, Government of Kerala, Thiruvanthapuram, 2000, p. 86.
55. Kutty, op. cit., p. 46.
56. Menon, op. cit., p. 14.
57. T.K. Gopala Panikkar, *Storm and Sunshine . . .*, p. 1.
58. Diary of M.A. Candeth, dated 8 January 1909.
59. Abigail McGowan, 'Consuming Families: Negotiating Women's Shopping in Early Twentieth Century Western India' in Douglas E. Haynes et al., eds., *Towards a History of Consumption in South Asia*, Oxford University Press, New Delhi, 2010, pp. 155-84.
60. 'Bharthakanmarude Vishamasthidhi', unsigned article, *Vijayan*, vol. 2, no. 7, August 1938, p. 17.
61. Prashant Kidambi, 'Consumption, Domestic Economy and the Idea of the Middle Class in late Colonial Bombay' in Douglas E. Haynes et al., eds., *Towards a History of Consumption in South Asia*, Oxford University Press, New Delhi, 2010, pp. 118-19.
62. The food habits of the people changed under the impact of colonialism. Even the Nambudiris, the most traditional amongst the different communities of Malabar, succumbed to these changes. As a contemporary observer put it, 'when tobacco first made its appearance, the Brahmins used to wash themselves after so far as touching it. . . . Now, even a *Shradha* ceremony would not be complete without chewing tobacco in the end. . . . As for tea and coffee, there would be very few Brahmins who have not yet started on them.' C.S. Subramanya Potti, 'Aachara Parishkarathinte Aavishyakatha-2', *Aatmaposhini*, vol. 6, no. 9, 1916, pp. 231-4. The changes, interestingly, brought forth criticism from some Europeans. Fawcett commented that, 'as the old order changeth giving place to new . . . it is truly sad to read of the celebration of a *Sambandham* ceremony at Calicut where there was cake and wine for the guests, and a ring for the bride. The departure from national and therefore rational custom for adoption of that which is neither custom nor ceremonial when copied meaninglessly is surely food for painful reflection.' F. Fawcett, *Nayars of Malabar*, Superindendent of Government Press, Madras, p. 64.
63. R. Iswara Pillai, 'Nammude Parishkaram', p. 13.
64. In the early twentieth century, coffee became popular among the Indians. A.R. Venkatachalapathy shows how it soon became a sign of the modern in Chennai, replacing traditional drinks. But, he also points out how this encounter led to a cultural anxiety regarding the

dangers the drink posed to the Tamil's physical and cultural health. A.R. Venkatachalapathy, 'In Those Days there was no Coffee: Coffee-Drinking and Middle-Class Culture in Colonial Tamil Nadu', in *In Those Days There was No Coffee: Writings in Cultural History*, Yoda Press, New Delhi, 2006, pp. 11-31.

65. M. Kesavan Vaidyan, 'Anukaranam, Athu Arogya Vishayathil Konduvarunna Doshangal', *Mathrubhoomi*, vol. 11, no. 50, March 1934, p. 27.
66. *Sreeman Murkoth Kumarante Sashtipoorthi Aaghosha Vivaram*, Imperial Printing Works, Tellicherry, 1934, p. 100.
67. Ibid.
68. Changarakumarath Sankaran, *C. Krishnan*, Sidhartha Book House, Trichur, 1967, p. 31. Attempts at abolition was especially strong among the emergent middle classes in the Thiyya community represented by people like C. Krishnan, for whom there was an urgent need to get rid of the stigma attached to toddy-making in which a significant section of the community had been involved in the past. Later, in fact, there were attempts to prove that, in the past, the Thiyyas, at least a majority of them were not involved in toddy-tapping, but instead were engaged in other pursuits including teaching, medicine, and even martial duties. See for instance, A. Aiyappan, *Iravas and Cultural Change*, Bulletin of the Madras Museum, New Series, vol. V, no. I, Government Press, Madras, 1944.
69 Sankaran, op. cit., p. 31.
70. *Kerala Patrika*, 11 May 1889 in NNPR for the week ending 31 May 1889, p. 107.
71. K.V.N. Gurukkal, 'Madhyavarjanam', *Mathrubhumi Weekly*, vol. 15, no. 52, 14 March 1938, p. 25.
72. S.A. Azariah, 'The Problem of Drink', in *The Malabar Quarterly Review*, vol. X, no. I, March 1911, pp. 41-2.
73. Sanjayan, 'Injection', *Sanjayante Theranhedutha Lekhanangal*, Poorna Publications, Kozhikode, 2006, pp. 16-21.
74. E.M.S. Namboodiripad, *Atmakatha*, Chintah Publishers, Trivandrum, 1985, p. 25.
75. *Kerala Patrika,* 5 April 1912 in NNPR for the week ending 12 April 1913, p. 593.
76. P.S. Varriar, *Dhanwantari*, 14 May 1917 cited in K.N. Panikkar, 'Indigenous Medicine and Cultural Hegemony: A Study of the Revitalization Movement in Keralam, *Studies in History*, 8,2, n.s. (1992), p. 298.
77. Samuel Aaron, 'Ayurveda Oushadangalum Chikilsamurakalum', *Mathrubhumi*, vol. 23, no. 23, 19 August 1945, p. 8.

78. Joshi, op. cit., p. 4.
79. *Report of The Malabar Marriage Commission*, p. 4.
80. Ibid., pp. 4-5.
81. S. Menon Marath, *The Wound of Spring*, Malayalam tr. M. Gangadhara Menon, Poorna Publictaions, Kozhikode, 1997 (1st pub. 1960).
82. Partha Chatterjee, 'A Religion of Urban Domesticity: Sri Ramakrishna and the Calcutta Middle Class' in P. Chatterjee, G. Pandey, eds., *Subaltern Studies*, vol. VII, Oxford University Press, New Delhi, 1992,.
83. O. Chandu Menon, *Indulekha*, DC Books, Kottayam, 2010 (1st pub. 1889), pp. 189-225.
84. Murkoth Kumaran, *Thiyyarude Nila*, Kannur Printing Works, Kannur, 1934, pp. 16-18.
85. Janaki Ram, *V.K. Krishna Menon: A Personal Memoir*, Oxford University Press, New Delhi, 1997, pp. xiii-xiv.
86. Kainikkara M. Kumara Pillai, *Malaylam Literary Survey*, January 1977.
87. Janaki Ram, op. cit., p. 14.
88. Karthiyanikutti Amma, *Thirumumbinoppam*, Chintha Publishers, Thiruvanthapuram, 2006, p. 50.
89. Panikkar, op. cit., This hybridization is also reflected in the process whereby indigenous cleansing agents combined with modern industries to produce the modern soap in the country as Indian companies like Godrej successfully competed with the foreign ones in a growing market for the product. The use of vegetable oils in their products in consideration of Indian sentiments as against the animal fats used by the foreign companies was one strategic device employed by the indigenous enterprises during this phase. Harminder Kaur, 'Of Soaps and Scents: Corporeal Cleanliness in Urban Colonial India', in Douglas E. Haynes, et al., eds., op. cit., p. 254.
90. Keezhedath Vasudevan Nair, *Vaidyaratnam P.S. Variar*, P.M. Variar Managing Trustee, Kottakal, 1953, p. 161.

Conclusion

In the preceding pages, through the writings available for the period, we tried to unravel the social history of the middle class in colonial Malabar. It was the administrative changes during the colonial period which provided the backdrop to the emergence of the new middle class. Government offices and the courts provided the arena where the educated natives could hope to find employment. When the sale of land became common following the break down of *tarawads*, and marriages began to be registered, registration offices became a reality. The spread of education witnessed from the late nineteenth century onwards resulted in the creation of several hundreds of school and college teachers who became an important segment of the middle class.

The middle class is not a homogeneous group. Within it, one will find those who are so well off that it would not be inappropriate to tag them along with the upper class; on the other hand, there are those who, in their lifestyle and values, would resemble the working class. This is why, then, certain scholars have talked of the 'middle classes' rather than the 'middle class'. In this book, the two phrases are used interchangeably. Two features that characterized all members of the group in Malabar during the colonial period had been their opposition towards the class of landlords, and the constant vigil to keep themselves segregated from the working class below them.

Though in the initial stages, the middle class was not dominant numerically, its influence was significant all along. The middle class had become the custodians of dominant cultural values in a society undergoing rapid transition. This was possible due to the knowledge the group possessed, mostly through Western education, and its ability to communicate it.

An important area where the middle class' presence was evident, and through which it established a stranglehold over the realm of culture was the press. What began in the middle of the nineteenth century had acquired phenomenal growth by the early twentieth century. Missionary publications cohabited and competed with caste publications and the nationalist press.

Malayalam had evolved into a modern language by then. And, through it, new modes of writing became possible. The novel, very much a genre of the new middle class, was the most important among them. Beginning with O. Chandu Menon's *Indulekha*, many novels, mostly reflecting middle-class lives, achieved stunning success.[1] Other types of writing include the short story and, of course, the 'autobiography', which was one of the most self-conscious of middle-class literary expressions. In fact, these autobiographies, some of them written by women, as well as diaries, provide some of the most important sources to access the psyche of the middle class in colonial Malabar.

The public sphere, including the press, was dominated by men. Though there were the odd writings by women in the magazines of the time, they did not represent a contestation to the prevailing patriarchal norms. This could well be said of some of the women's associations that sprang up during this time as well. Their functioning was strictly in conformity with the gendered roles women were expected to play. And, when the odd deviations from the prescribed path took place, satirists like Sanjayan were quick to pounce on them. Even as men dominated the public sphere, the 'home' was designated as the realm where the woman was expected to hold sway. Here, she was expected to raise children and perform her wifely duties to perfection. There were calls during this time for women's education to be re-structured to suit her role at home. Though theoretically, women controlled the home, in practise, men continued to dictate terms. Laws strengthened the position of the father, as did the literature of the times. Women's financial dependence on their men ensured their subordinate status at home.

Home was valorized by the middle class as a haven from the troubles outside it. An ideal family living in it was to consist of the husband, wife and their children. The nuclear family had become a possibility following the disintegration of the *tarawads*, and laws which brought into existence legal forms of marriage. Romantic love, which makes its appearance in the literature of the period, strengthened the union between the husband and the wife. Photography, a recent invention, kept alive the memory of family members who were no more, as well as of important occasions in the family.

Leisure took new forms during this time. Religious functions which passed off as entertainments in the past gave way to new secular ones. Now, within home, one important way to spend time constituted reading which was, in no small measure, helped by the spread of education and literacy. And, with the proliferation of publications, there was sufficient reading to be had. Of the literature available, secular prose attracted readers the most; spiritual poems, which was the main component of literature in an earlier era, now, catered to a minority. Radio provided information as well as entertainment. Some took to gardening, while others engaged themselves with the interior decoration of their house.

The growing belief during this period was that physical activities kept the body and mind healthy. There was, as a consequence, a proliferation of games, of which cricket became one of the most popular. With the introduction of modern means of transport, travelling for pleasure became a possibility. Circus, with its roots in north Malabar, provided entertainment to many.

However, of all the different forms of entertainment, it was cinema which captured the imagination of the people the most. Though there were misgivings in some quarters regarding its possible dangers, the general consensus was that its benefits out-weighed them. The middle class, inspite of flocking to the halls in large numbers to view a movie, kept a distance from its production process, including acting, which did not acquire respectability until recent times. And, inside the cinema halls, separate enclosures meant that those who could afford higher-priced tickets will not have to sit alongside the lower classes.

Among the Hindus, the middle classes came from all the castes. However, the financially less privileged among the Nairs and the slightly well-off among the Thiyyas, who went for Western education, dominated. The rich Nairs and the Nambudiris, in general, took time to adjust to the rapid changes taking place around them, and, in the process, got left behind. In the new workplace and in the public arena, the earlier legitimacy enjoyed by caste got eroded. The cosmopolitan lifestyle which the newly emergent cities made possible did not give much space for caste to thrive. Railways further eroded the barriers between people and regions. Privileges based on birth now counted for less. Public-spirited individuals organized inter-dining. A few intercaste marriages took place; and, several friendships cutting across caste faultlines were forged. People began to give up their caste-markers which, in an earlier era, had helped people identify different castes – and behave accordingly – in a highly hierarchized society. But the vestiges of the past persisted in the minds of a few, and at a deeply personal level, caste continued to play a significant role.

With regard to colonial modernity too, the attitude of the middle class remained ambivalent. There was, by no means, a clearly-defined conflict between tradition and modernity. The approach, as the class grew in maturity, was to filter and selectively imbibe from Western civilization what was best for the native society, while remaining rooted in one's own tradition. Those who blindly imitated the West were ridiculed, and the few who rejected modernity in toto got themselves sidelined from the progress the state was to witness in the decades to follow.

* * *

The world has changed dramatically since 1947. Malabar as a political unit no longer exists. In 1956, it merged with Travancore and Cochin to form the modern Kerala state. Meanwhile, following developments over the years, not least the liberalization of the 1990s, there has been a huge increase in the number of middle-class Indians across the country, especially so in Kerala. Of the approximate 240 million middle-class citizens in the country, around 16.7 million live in Kerala. Caste reservation by state and central governments has ensured adequate middle-class representation from amongst the lower castes as well.

The Gulf boom from the 1970s made many Malayali families affluent. Kerala gets one trillion rupees in the form of remittances, most of which, however, is spent on the construction of palatial houses, cars and consumer goods. Consequently, there has been no visible industrialization, and unemployment remains high. Like in the pre-Independence era, the middle classes are constituted mainly by those working in the service sector and the professionals. Despite the lack of economic growth, social movements and government policies have enabled the state to possess the best social and human development indexes in the country, with the highest life expectancy and the lowest infant mortality figures. The average Malayali continues to abhor doing manual work as a result of which there has been a huge influx of migrant labourers into the state from the north and eastern parts of the country in recent years to fill up that lacunae.

Seven decades have passed since the period of our study ended. The years have brought with them changes in all spheres of life including the ways in which people spend their leisure. Circus is nearly dead while cricket has flourished, and the state now produces players of international calibre. FM stations have kept the radio alive, but its place in middle class living rooms have long since been taken over by the TV sets, while mobile phones have diminished the valued of print culture. Transport has advanced dramatically; railways have expanded, but many amongst the middle classes now have cars, and can afford to travel by air. However, some things have remained unchanged. There was a moment in the immediate aftermath of Independence, and the establishment of the first communist ministry later, when the ideals of modernity seemed to have reigned supreme. Astrology, among other superstitions, had become unfashionable. But if the recent Sabarimala stir is anything to go by, tradition still holds sway in the minds of the middle class. Caste movements which once played an important role in the democratization of society, today, for the most part, have become epicentres of vested interests. Statistics on women remain an anomaly. While the state boasts of a sex ratio in favour of women, higher life expectancy for them compared to men, and low maternal mortality, it occupies the lowest position in the country as far as their presence in the workforce is concerned and leadership positions in different fields.

That is the present. But, you can find anticipations of the present in the past. That is precisely what this book has tried to unravel while reconstructing the social history of the middle class in colonial Malabar. In the process, we came across characters who appear somewhat familiar as earlier versions of our present selves. The past, thus, lives on in the present.

NOTE

1. Novels written by the middle-class authors on the lives of the subaltern classes were to emerge from the 1930s with the rise of the Communist movement.

Glossary

Adda	the Bengali term for chatting
Anantharavan	nephew
Antarjanam	women belonging to the Nambudiri community
Bhadralok	the Bengali equivalent of a gentleman
Grihabharanam	household management
Illam	household of a Nambudiri Brahmin
Janmi	one possessing hereditary rights over land
Karanavan	male head of the household
Karyasthan	manager
Kathaprasangam	story-telling performance
Kuduma	long hair on the head tied in a knot
Mallikhana	pension given by the British to ex-princes
Mangalapatram	lyrical Best Wishes
Marumakkathayam	matriliny
Mundu	garment around the waist
Munshi	language teacher
Nalukettu	traditional homestead in Kerala
Nattezhuthachhanmar	traditional teachers
Nayattu	hunting
Nigandu	lexicon
Punool	sacred thread
Sambandham	loose customary marriage
Shastipoorthi	sixtieth birthday
Smarthavicharam	ritualistic trial of a Nambudiri woman and her male sexual partner(s) for adultery
Thalikettu Kalyanam	ritual on attaining puberty
Tarawad	ancestral home

Utsavams	festivals in temples
Vakil	lawyer
Yogakshemam	Nambudiri community reform movement
Zamorin	the English variant of Samoodiri, the ruler of Calicut

Bibliography

Primary Sources

(a) *English Fiction and Non-Fiction*

Das, Kamala, *A Childhood in Malabar*, tr. Gita Krishnankutty, Penguin, New Delhi, 2003.

Dunsterville, F., *Illustrated Guide to the Madras Railway*, Higgin-botham and Co., Madras, 1898.

Fawcett, F., *Nayars of Malabar*, Superintendent of Government Press, Madras, 1915.

Kutty, P.K.S., *Years of Laughter: Reminiscences of a Cartoonist*, Thema, Kolkata, 2009.

Nair, C. Sankaran, *Autobiography of Chettur Sankaran Nair*, Chettur Sankaran Nair Foundation, Ottapalam, 1998 (1st pub. 1966).

Nambiar, B.Govindan, *Handbook of Malabar Law and Usage as Administered by the Courts*, ALV Press, Madras, 1899.

Namboodiri, P.S., *A Handbook of Physical Activities*, Mangalodayam Press, Trichur, 1935.

Panikkar, T.K. Gopala, *Malabar and its Folk*, G.A. Natesan and Company, Madras, 1901.

Panikkar, T.K. Gopala, *Storm and Sunshine: A Novel Illustrative of Malayalee Domestic Life*, the Norman Printing Bureau, Calicut, 1916.

Ram, Janaki, *V.K. Krishna Menon: A Personal Memoir*, Oxford University Press, New Delhi, 1997.

(b) *Malayalam Fiction and Non-Fiction*

Amma, C.K. Revathy, *Sahasra Poornima*, Vidyavilasam Press, Tellicherry, 1977.

Amma, Karthiyanikutti, *Thirumumbinoppam*, Chintha Publishers, Thiruvanthapuram, 2006.

Balamaniamma, *Ammayude Lokam*, (essays written earlier), Priya Publishers, Trichur, 1982.

———, *Jeevithathilude*, Mathrubhumi Printing and Publishing Co. Ltd., Kozhikode, 1969.

Bhattadiripad, M.P., *Rhuthumathy*, Current Books, Trichur, 1991 (1st pub. 1944).

Bhattathirippad, V.T., *VT yude Sampoorna Kruthikal*, DC Books, Kottayam, 2006.

Cherukad, *Jeevithapadha*, Current Books, Trichur, 2003 (1st pub. 1974).

Kesavan, C., *Jeevithasamaram*, DC Books, Kottayam, 2010 (1st pub. 1968).

Kumaran, Murkoth, *Ammamarodu*, Kerala State Council for Child Welfare, Trivandrum, 1977 (1st pub. 1927).

———, *Oyarath Chandu Menon*, Kerala Sahitya Akademi, Trichur, 1996 (1st pub. 1932).

———, *Thiyyarude Nila*, Kannur Printing Works, Kannur, 1934.

———, *Vasumati*, Sriramavilasam Press, Kollam, 1935.

Kunhappa, C.H., *Smaranakal Matram*, Mathrubhumi Press, Kozhikode, 1981.

Kunhappa, Murkoth, *Murkoth Kumaran*, Sahitya Pravarthaka Co-operatrive Society Ltd., Kottayam, 1975.

Marath, S. Menon, *The Wound of Spring* [1960], Malayalam tr., M. Gangadhara Menon, Poorna Publications, Kozhikode, 1997.

Menon, K.P. Kesava, *Bilathi Visesham*, Mathrubhumi Books, Kozhikode, 2007 (1st pub. 1916).

———, *Kazhinja Kaalam*, The Mathrubhumi Printing and Publishing Company Limited, Calicut, 1986 (1st pub. 1957).

Menon, Kizhakkepattu Ramankutty, *Parangodeeparinayam* DC Books, Kottayam, 2004 (1st pub. 1892),.

Menon, M.P. Sivadasa, *Malabarile Sikkaru*, DC Books, Kottayam, 2002 (1st pub. 1959).

Menon, O. Chandu, *Indulekha*, DC Books, Kottayam, 2010 (1st pub. 1889).

———, *Sarada*, DC Books, Kottayam, 2008 (1st pub. 1892).

Menon, Variath Balakrishna, *Premabandham*, Durgalaya Press, Cochin, 1917.

Musathu, K.V., *Atmakatha*, National Book Stall, Kottayam, 1966.

Nair, C. Chathu, *Meenakshi*, B.V. Book Depot, Thiruvanthapuram, 1949.

Nair, K. Kannan, *Atmakatha*, Mathrubhumi Publishing House, Calicut, 1989.

Nair, K.M., *Muliyil Krishnan*, Norman Printing Bureau, Calicut, 1932.

Nair, Keezhedath Vasudevan, *Vaidyaratnam P.S. Variar*, P.M. Variar Managing Trustee, Kottakal, 1953.

Nair, P. Kunhanandan (Thikkodiyan), *Arangu Kanatha Nadan*, DC Books, Kottayam, 2008.

Nair, P. Narayanan, *Ara Nootandilude*, Kerala Sahitya Akademi, Trichur, 1973.

Namboodiripad, E.M.S., *Atmakatha*, Chintah Publishers, Trivandrum, 1985.

Namboodirippad, Mozhikunnathu Brahmadathan, *Khilafath Smaranakal*, Mathrubhumi Books, 2010 (1st pub. 1965).

Namputiripattu, K.S., *Ente Smaranakal*, vol. I, Panchangam Book House, Kunnamkulam, 1963.

Nayanar, Kesari Vengayil Kunhiraman, *Prabhandangalum, Kathakalum Mattum*, Bharatavilasam Press, 1956.

Nayanar, V.R., ed., *Malabar Vidyabyasa Guide*, Mathrubhumi, Kozhikode, 1939.

Nayanar, Vengayil Kunhiraman, *Kesari Nayanarude Krithikal*, Mathrubhumi Printing and Publishing Company Limited, Calicut, 1987.

Sanjayan, *Sanjayante Theranhedutha Lekhanangal*, Poorna Publications, Kozhikode, 2006.

Sankaran, Changarakumarath, *C. Krishnan*, Sidhartha Book House, Trichur, 1967.

Sankaran, Moyarath., *Ente Jivitha Katha*, P.K. Brothers, Calicut, 1965.

Sreeman Murkoth Kumarante Sashtipoorthi Aaghosha Vivaram, Imperial Printing Works, Tellicherry, 1934.

(c) *Diaries (NMML, New Delhi)*

G. Sankaran Nair.

K.P.S. Menon.

M.A. Candeth.

(d) *English Journals*

BEMP School Magazine (1941-7).

BGM College Magazine (1912).

Government Brennen College Magazine (1931-9).

Malabar Christian College Magazine (1932-47).

Malabar Quarterly Review (1904-11).

The Teacher's Magazine (1941).
Zamorin's College Magazine (1912-47).

(e) *Malayalam Journals*

Aatmaposhini (1910-16).
Dharmaprabha (1933).
Gurukulam (1924-6).
Gurunathan (1921).
Kairali (1916-18).
Mangalodayam (1908-30).
Mathrubhumi (1932-47).
Mitavadi (1913-30).
Murali (1933-4).
Sanjayan (1936).
Unni Nambuthiri (1918-29).
Vijayan (1938).
Viswaroopam (1940).
Vivekodayam (1904-6).

(f) *English Newspapers (Tamil Nadu State Archives)*

Native Newspaper Reports (1880-1920).

(g) *Government Documents* (National Archives of India, Tamil Nadu State Archives, Kozhikode Regional Archives)

Census of India (1881-1941).

First Tour of H.E. The Right Hon. Lord Pentland, Governor of Madras (Coimbatore and Malabar), Government Press, Madras, 1913.

Graeme, H.S., *Graeme's Glossary*, Government Press, Madras, 1982.

Innes, C.A., *Malabar Gazetteer*, Government Press, Madras, 1951(1st pub. 1908).

Logan, William, *Malabar*, vol. I, Asian Educational Services, New Delhi, 1989 (1st pub. 1887).

Report of the Malabar Marriage Commission, Lawrence Asylum Press, Madras, 1891.

Report on Public Instruction in the Madras Presidency (for some years ranging from 1875 to 1925).

Statement of Population of 1871 in Each Village of the Malabar District Arranged According to Area, Caste and Occupation, Govt. Gazette Press, Madras, 1874.

Statistical Atlas of Malabar, 1906.

Thorne, J.A., *Report on the Zamorin's Estate*, Collectorate Press, Madras, 1913.

Secondary Sources

(a) *English*

Allen, Michell, ed., *Bourgeois Society in Nineteenth Century Europe*, Berg Publishers, Oxford, 1993.

Anderson, Nels, *Man's Work and Leisure*, E. J. Brill, Leiden, 1974.

Arunima, G., 'Glimpses from a Writer's World: O. Chandu Menon, His Contemporaries, and Their Times', *Studies in History*, 20, 2, n.s. (2004).

________, 'Multiple Meanings: Changing Conceptions of Matrilineal Kinship in Nineteenth and Twentieth Century Malabar', *The Indian Economic and Social History Review*, 33, 3 (1996).

________, *There Comes Papa: Colonialism and the Transformation of Matriliny in Kerala, Malabar c.1850-1940*, Orient Longman, New Delhi, 2003.

Awasthy, G.C., *Broadcasting in India*, Allied Publishers Private Limited, Bombay, 1965.

Bagchi, Jasodara 'Representing Nationalism: Ideology and Motherhood in Colonial Bengal', Review of Women's Studies, *Economic and Political Weekly*, 20-7 October, 1990.

Balan, C., 'Political Economy of Transport Infrastructure Development in Kerala during the Colonial Period', in C. Balan, ed., *Reflections on Malabar: Society, Institution and Culture*, The Post-Graduate Department of History, Nehru Arts and Science College, Kanhangad, 2000.

Banerjea, Surendranath, *A Nation in the Making*, Oxford University Press, New Delhi, 1963 (1st pub. 1925).

Banerjee, Sumanta, *The Parlour and the Streets: Elite and Popular Culture in Nineteenth Century Calcutta*, Seagull Books, Calcutta, 1998 (1st pub. 1989).

________, 'The West turned "Upside Down" in a Bengali Satire' in C. Vijayasree, ed., *Writing the West: Representations from Indian Languages*, Sahitya Akademi, New Delhi, 2004.

Banerjee, Swapna M., 'Child, Mother, Servant: Motherhood and

Domestic Ideology in Colonial Bengal', in Avril A. Powell and Siobhan Lambert-Hurley, eds., *Rhetoric and Reality: Gender and the Colonial Experience in South Asia*, Oxford University Press, New Delhi, 2006.

Bates, Crispin, ed., *Beyond Representation: Colonial and Postcolonial Constructions of Indian Identity*, Oxford University Press, New Delhi, 2006.

Bayly, C.A., *Indian Society and the Making of the British Empire*, Cambridge University Press, Cambridge, 1988.

Beteille, Andre 'Caste in Contemporary India', in C.J. Fuller, *Caste Today*, Oxford University Press, New Delhi, 1996.

________, 'The Social Character of the Indian Middle Class' in Imtiaz Ahmad et al., eds., *Middle Class Values in India and Western Europe*, Social Science Press, New Delhi, 2002.

Bhattacharya, Tithi, *The Sentinels of Culture: Class, Education, and the Colonial Intellectual in Bengal (1848-85)*, Oxford University Press, New Delhi, 2005.

Bose, Pradeep, 'Sons of the Nation', in Partha Chatterjee, ed., *Texts of Power: Emerging Disciplines in Colonial Bengal*, University of Minnesota Press, Minneapolis, 1995.

Bose, Pradip Kumar, 'Reconstituting Private Life: The Making of the Modern Family in Bengal', in Ghanshyam Shah, ed., *Social Transformation in India*, vol. 2, Rawat Publications, New Delhi, 1997.

Brosius, Christiane, *India's Middle Class: New Forms of Urban Leisure, Consumption and Prosperity*, Routledge, New Delhi, 2010.

Caillois, Roger, *Man, Play and Games*, Free Press, New York, 1961.

Cannadine, David, *Class in Britain*, Yale University Press, London, 1998.

________, *History in Our Time*, Yale University Press, London, 1998.

Chakravarty, Dipesh, 'Open Space/Public Place: Garbage, Modernity and India', *South Asia*,vol. XIV, no.1 (1991).

________, *Provincialising Europe: Postcolonial Thought and Historical Difference*, Princeton University Press, Princeton, 2000.

________, 'The Difference Deferral of a Colonial Modernity: Public Debates on Domesticity in British India', in David Arnold and David Hardiman, eds., *Subaltern Studies VIII: Essays in Honour of Ranajit Guha*, Oxford University Press, New Delhi, 1994.

Chatterjee, Partha, 'A Religion of Urban Domesticity: Sri Ramakrishna and the Calcutta Middle Class' in P. Chatterjee and G. Pandey, eds., *Subaltern Studies*, vol. VII, Oxford University Press, 1992.

________, *The Nation and its Fragments: Colonial and Postcolonial Histories*, Princeton University Press, Princeton, 1993.

———, 'The Nationalist Resolution of the Women's Question', in K. Sanghari and S. Vaid, eds., *Recasting Women: Essays in Colonial History*, Kali for Women, Delhi, 1988.

Chibbar, Y.P., *From Caste to Class: A Study of the Indian Middle Classes*, Associated Publishing House, New Delhi, 1968.

Cohn, Bernard, *An Anthropologist among the Historians and Other Essays*, Delhi, Oxford University Press, 1970.

———, *Colonialism and its Forms of Knowledge*, Oxford University Press, New Delhi, 1997.

Dann, R. 'The Urban Geography of Malabar', *The Journal of the Madras Geographical Association*, vol. VI, nos. 3&4, October 1931-January 1932.

Dasgupta, Sanjukta and Malashri Lal, ed., *The Indian Family in Transition: Reading Literary and Cultural Texts*, Sage, New Delhi, 2007.

Davis, Kingley, *The Population of India and Pakistan*, Princeton University Press, Princeton, 1951.

Devika, J., *Her-Self: Early Writings on Gender by Malayalee Women, 1898-1938*, Stree, Kolkata, 2005.

———, *Individuals, Householders Citizens: Malayalis and Family Planning, 1930-1970*, Zubaan, New Delhi, 2008.

———, 'Negotiating Women's Social Space: Public Debates on Gender in Early Modern Kerala, India', *Inter-Asia Cultural Studies*, vol. 7, no. 1, 2006.

Dirks, Nicholas, *The Hollow Crown: Ethnohistory of an Indian Kingdom*, Cambridge University Press, Cambridge, 1987.

Dumazedier, Joffre, *Toward a Society of Leisure*, (tr. Stewart E. McClure), Free Press, New York, 1967.

Dumont, Louis, *Homo Hierarchicus: The Caste System and its Implications*, University of Chicago Press, Chicago, 1980.

Embree, Ainslee T., 'Land Holding in India and British Institutions', in Robert E. Frykenberg, ed., *Land Control and Social Structure in Indian History*, Manohar, New Delhi, 1979.

Ganguli, B.N. 'Conceptualising the Indian Middle Class', in K.S. Krishnaswamy, Asok Mitra, I.G. Patel, K.N. Raj and M.N. Srinivas, *Essays in Honour of Sachin Choudhury*, Oxford University Press, Bombay, 1977.

Crossick, Geoffrey and Heinz-Gerhard Haupt, *The Petite Bourgeoisie in Europe 1780-1914, Enterprise, Family and Independence*, Routledge, London, 1995.

Ganesh, K.N., ed., *Culture and Modernity: Historical Explorations*, University of Calicut, Calicut, 2004.

Gest, N.P. and S.F. Fava, *Urban Society*, Crowell, New York, 1964.

Ghosh, Anindita 'Identities Made in Print: Literary Bengali and its 'Others', *c.*1800-1905', in Crispin Bates, ed., *Beyond Representation: Colonial and Postcolonial Constructions of Indian Identity*, Oxford University Press, New Delhi, 2006.

Ginsberg, Morris, 'Class Consciousness', in *Encyclopedia of the Social Sciences,* Macmillan, New York, 1957.

Gough, Kathleen E., 'Variations in Matrilineal Systems', in David Schneider and Kathleen E. Gough, eds., *Matrilineal Kinship*, University of California Press, Berkeley, 1961.

Habermas, Jurgen, *The Structural Transformation of the Public Sphere: An Inquiry into a Category of Bourgeois Society*, (tr. Thomas Burger), MIT Press, Cambridge, 1991.

Hall, Catherine, 'The Sweet Delights of Home', in Michelle Perrot, ed., *A History of Private Life*, vol. IV: *From the Fires of Revolution to the Great War*, Harvard University Press, Cambridge, Massachusetts, 1990.

Hall, Catherine, *White, Male and Middle Class: Explorations in Feminism and History*, Polity Press, London, 1992.

Haynes, Douglas E. et al., eds., *Towards a History of Consumption in South Asia*, Oxford University Press, New Delhi, 2010.

Hesterlow, A.M.V., 'Public Health of Malabar in Relation to Environment', *The Journal of the Madras Geographical Association*, vol.VI, nos. 3&4, October 1931-January 1932.

Hobsbawm, Eric 'The Example of the English Middle Class', in Jurgen Kocka and Allan Mitchell, eds., *Bourgeois Society in Nineteenth Century Europe,* Berg Publishers, Oxford, 1993.

James, Lawrence, *The Middle Class: A History,* Little Brown, London, 2006.

Jeffrey, Robin 'Governments and Culture: How Women made Kerala Literate', *Pacific Affairs*, vol. 60, no. 3, Fall 1987.

________, *India's Newspaper Revolution: Capitalism, Politics and the Indian-Language Press*, Oxford University Press, New Delhi, 2010.

Joshi, Sanjay, *Fractured Modernity: Making of a Middle Class in Colonial North India*, Oxford University Press, New Delhi, 2001.

________, ed., *The Middle Class in Colonial India*, Oxford University Press, New Delhi, 2010.

Joyce, Patrick, *Visions of the People: Industrial England and the Question of Class, 1840-1914*, Cambridge University Press, Cambridge, 1992.

Karlekar, Malavika., *Re-visioning the Past: Early Photography in Bengal, 1875-1915*, Oxford University Press, New Delhi.

Kaur, Harminder, 'Of Soaps and Scents: Corporeal Cleanliness in Urban

Colonial India', in Douglas E. Haynes et al., eds., *Towards a History of Consumption in South Asia*, Oxford University Press, New Delhi, 2010.

Kaviraj, Sudipta, *The Unhappy Consciousness: Bankimchandra Chattopadhyay and the Formation of Nationalist Discourse in India*, Oxford University Press, 1993.

Kidambi, Prashant, 'Consumption, Domestic Economy and the Idea of the Middle Class in late Colonial Bombay', in Douglas E. Haynes et al., eds., *Towards a History of Consumption in South Asia*, Oxford University Press, New Delhi, 2010.

Kodoth, Praveena, 'Courting Legitimacy or Delegitimizing Custom?: Sexuality, Sambandham, and Marriage Reform in Late Nineteenth Century Malabar', in *Modern Asian Studies*, 35, 2 (2001).

________, 'Shifting the Ground of Fatherhood: Matriliny, Men and Marriage in Early Twentieth Century Malabar', CDS Working Paper, May 2004.

Lewandowsky, Susan, *Migration and Ethnicity in Urban India: Kerala Migrants in the City of Madras 1870-1970*, Manohar, New Delhi, 1970.

Lundberg, George A. et al., *Leisure: A Suburban Study*, Columbia University Press, New York, 1934.

Mackintosh-Smith, Tim, *Travels with a Tangerine: A Journey in the Footsteps of Ibn Batutah*, Picador, London, 2002.

Majumdar, Boria, 'A Case of Indian Exceptionalism: Bengali Middle Class Patronage of Sport in Colonial Bengal', in Sanjay Joshi, ed., *The Middle Class in Colonial India*, Oxford University Press, New Delhi, 2010.

Manmathan, M.R. 'Introspecting Nambutiri Reform in Kerala: Reflections on Ulbudhakeralam', *History Farook Series*, No. 2, November 2006.

Mathew, George, *Communal Road to Secular Kerala*, Concept Publishing House, New Delhi, 1989.

Mayer, Adrian, *Land and Society in Malabar*, Oxford University Press, Bombay, 1952.

Mayer, Arnie J., 'The Lower Middle Class as Historical Problem', *Journal of Modern History*, 47, September 1975.

McCormack, Thelma 'Politics and Leisure', *International Journal of Comparative Sociology*, 12, no. 3, September 1971.

McGowan, Abigail, 'Consuming Families: Negotiating Women's Shopping in Early Twentieth Century Western India' in Douglas E. Haynes et al., eds., *Towards a History of Consumption in South Asia*, Oxford University Press, New Delhi, 2010.

Mcguire, John, *The Making of a Colonial Mind: A Quantitative Study of the Bhadralok in Calcutta, 1857-1885*, Australian National University

Monograph on South Asia no. 10, Australian National University, 1983.

Mencher, Joan P., 'Kerala and Madras: A Comparative Study of Ecology and Social Structure, *Ethnology*, vol. V, no. 1, January 1976.

————, 'The Nayars of South Malabar', in M.F. Nimcoff, ed., *Comparative Family Systems*, Houghton Mifflin, Boston, 1965.

————, 'Changing Familial Roles among Malabar Nayars', *South Western Journal of Anthropology*, 18: 3, Autumn 1962.

Mencher, Joan P. and Helen Goldberg, 'Kinship and Marriage Regulations among the Namboodiri Brahmans of Kerala', *Man*, 2:1, (n.s.), March, 1967.

Menon, Dilip M., 'A Place Elsewhere: Lower-Caste Malayalam Novels of the Nineteenth Century', in Stuart Blackburn and Vasudha Dalmia, eds., *India's Literary History: Essays on the Nineteenth Century*, Permanent Black, Delhi, 2004.

————, 'Being a Brahmin the Marxist Way: E.M.S. Nambudiripad and the Pasts of Kerala', Daud Ali, ed., *Invoking the Past: The Uses of History in South Asia*, Oxford University Press, New Delhi, 1999.

————, 'Caste and Modernity: Reading Saraswati Vijayam', *Studies in History*, 13, 2, n.s., 1997.

Menon, Dilip M., *Caste, Nationalism and Communism in South India: Malabar 1900-1948*, Cambridge University Press, Cambridge, 1994.

Menon, K.P.S., ed., *Kesava Menon 90*, K.P. Kesava Menon 90th Birthday Celebration Committee, Calicut, 1977.

Misra, B.B., *The Indian Middle Classes: Their Growth in Modern Times*, Oxford University Press, New Delhi, 1978 (1st pub. 1961).

Misra, Tilottama, 'The Image of the West in Assamiya Literature', *Writing the West: Representations from Indian Languages*, Sahitya Akademi, New Delhi, 2004.

Mitter, Partha, *Art and Nationalism in Colonial India: 1850 -1922: Occidental Orientations*, Cambridge University Press, Cambridge, 1995.

Muralidharan, M., 'Hindu Community Formation in Kerala: Processes and Structures under Colonial Modernity, *South Indian Studies*, 2, July-December 1996.

Nair, R. Ramakrishnan, *The Middle Class in Kerala*, The Kerala Academy of Political Sciences, Trivandrum, 1974.

Nandy, Ashis, *An Ambiguous Journey to the City: The Village and other Odd Ruins of the Self in the Indian Imagination*, Oxford University Press, New Delhi, 2007.

Narayanan, M.G.S., 'Gods and Ancestors in Development: A Study of

Kerala', in M.A. Oommen, ed., *Rethinking Development: Kerala's Development Experience*, vol. I, Concept Publishing House, New Delhi, 1999.

Osella, Caroline and Filippo Osella, 'Once Upon a Time in the West: Narrating Modernity in Kerala, South India', in Jaqui Parry and David Arnold, eds., *Life Stories in South India*, Oxford University Press, New Delhi.

Padikkal, Shivarama, 'Inventing Modernity: The Emergence of the Novel in India', in Tejaswini Niranjana, P. Sudhir and Vivek Dhareshwar, eds., *Interrogating Modernity: Culture and Colonialism in India*, Seagull, Calcutta, 1993.

Pandian, M.S.S., 'One Step Outside Modernity: Caste in the Middle Class Imaginary', in Sanjay Joshi, ed., *The Middle Class in Colonial India*, Oxford University Press, New Delhi, 2010.

Panikkar, K.N. 'Creating a New Cultural Taste: Reading a Nineteenth Century Malayalam Novel', in *Culture, Ideology, Hegemony: Intellectuals and Social Consciousness in Colonial India*, Tulika, New Delhi, 1995.

————. 'Land Control, Ideology and Reform: A Study of the Changes in Family Organization and Marriage System in Kerala', *Indian Historical Review*, 4 (1), 1977.

————, 'Indigenous Medicine and Cultural Hegemony: A Study of the Revitalization Movement in Keralam, *Studies in History*, 8,2, n.s. (1992).

————, Agrarian Legislation and Social Classes: A Case Study of Malabar, *Economic and Political Weekly*, vol. 13, no. 21, 27 May 1978.

Parekh, Bhikhu, *Colonialism, Tradition and Reform: An Analysis of Gandhi's Political Discourse*, Sage, New Delhi, 1999.

Parker, Stanley, *The Sociology of Leisure*, George Allen & Unwin, London, 1976.

Prabhu, Balagopal T.S., 'Kerala Architecture', in P.J. Cherian, ed., *Essays on the Cultural Formation of Kerala: Literature, Art, Architecture, Music, Theatre, Cinema*, KCHR, Trivandrum, 1999.

Pullapilly, Cyriac K., 'The Izhavas of Kerala and their Historic Struggle for Acceptance in Kerala Society', in Bardwell L. Smith, ed., *Religion and Social Conflict in South Asia*, Brill, Leiden, 1976.

Raghaviah, Jayaprakash, *Basel Mission Industries in Malabar and South Canara 1834-1914: A Study of its Social and Economic Impact*, Gian Publishing House, New Delhi, 1990.

Rajeevan, B., 'From Caste to Sex: A Study on Sexuality and the Formation of Modern Subject in Kerala', in M.A. Oommen, ed., *Rethinking*

Development: Kerala's Development Experience, vol. I Concept Publishing House, New Delhi, 1999.

Ramachandran, T.K., 'Notes on the Making of Feminine Identity in Contemporary Kerala Society', *Social Scientist*, vol. 23, nos. 1-3, 1995.

Rao, M.S.A., *Social Change in Malabar*, the Popular Book Depot, Bombay, 1957.

Ray, Rajat Kanta, 'Political Change in British India', in *The Indian Economic and Social History Review*, vol. XIV, 1977.

________, *Exploring Emotional History: Gender, Mentality and Literature in the Indian Awakening*, Oxford University Press, New Delhi, 2001.

Raychaudhuri, Tapan, 'Love in a Colonial Climate: Marriage, Sex and Romance in Nineteenth Century Bengal', *Modern Asian Studies* (2000), 34.

Rothermund, Dietmar, *Indian Economy under British Rule and other Essays,* Manohar, New Delhi, 1983.

Roy, Tapti, 'Disciplining the Printed Text', in Chatterjee, Partha, ed., *Texts of Power: Emerging Disciplines in Colonial Bengal*, University of Minnesota Press, Minneapolis, 1995.

Saavala, Minna, *Middle Class Moralities: Everyday Struggle over Belonging and Prestige in India*, Orient Blackswan, New Delhi, 2010.

Sarkar, Sumit, *Writing Social History*, Oxford University Press, New Delhi, 1997.

________, *Modern Times: India 1880s-1950s*, Permanent Black, New Delhi, 2015.

Sarkar, Tanika, *Hindu Wife, Hindu Nation: Community, Religion and Cultural Nationalism,* Permanent Black, New Delhi, 2001.

Satchidanandan, K., 'Everyday and the Avant-Garde: The Contexts of Modernism in Malayalam Literature', in M.A. Oommen, ed., *Rethinking Development: Kerala's Development Experience*, vol. I, Concept Publishing House, New Delhi, 1999.

________, 'Renaissance, Decadence, Modernism and Post-modernism', Session 6, ICKS (International Congress on Kerala Studies)–A, vol. I, 1994.

________, 'Travel Writing in India: An Overview', in Shobhana Bhattacharji, ed., *Travel Writing in India*, Sahitya Akademi, New Delhi, 2008.

Sen, Simonti, *Travels to Europe: Self and other in Bengali Travel Narratives, 1870-1910*, Orient Longman, New Delhi, 2005.

Sheeba, K.M., 'From the Kitchen to the Stage and Back: Continuing Forms of Women's Exclusion in Keralam', in *Journal of South Indian History*, vol. 2, no. 2, March 2006.

Sreejith, K., 'Caste and the Middle Class in Colonial Malabar', *Bengal Past and Present*, vol. 133, 2014.

________, 'Domesticity in Colonial Malabar', *Bengal Past and Present*, vol. 128, 2009.

________, 'Leisure in Colonial Malabar', *Exploring History*, vol. III, no. 2, July-December 2012 and vol. IV, no. 1, January-June 2013 [combined vol.].

________, 'Negotiating Tradition and Modernity: Middle Class Dilemmas in Colonial Malabar', *Social Scientist*, vol. 41, nos. 3 & 4, March-April 2013.

Sreekumar, T.T., 'Urbanisation in Kerala, c. 1900-1981', M.Phil. dissertation, CDS, Trivandrum, 1988.

Srinivas, M.N., *Caste in Modern India and other Essays*, Asia Publishing House, Bombay, 1962.

Stearns, Peter N., *Childhood in World History*, Routledge, New York, 2006.

Subrahmanyam, N., 'A Note on the Transport and Communications in Malabar', *The Journal of the Madras Geographical Association*, vol. VI, nos. 3&4, October 1931-January 1932.

Tharakan, Michael, 'Migration from Travancore to Malabar 1930-1950', CDS Working Paper, no. 154.

Thomas, Ninan, 'Physical Education: What & Why', *Government Brennen College Magazine*, March 1931.

Torri, Michelguglielmo, '"Westernised Middle Class", Intellectuals and Society in Late Colonial India', *EPW*, 27 January 1990.

Tosh, John, 'The New Men: The Bourgeois Cult of Home', in *History Today*, 46, December 1996.

Unni, K. Raman, 'Visiting Husbands in Malabar', *Journal of the M.S. University of Baroda*, vol. 5, 1956.

Varma, Pavan K., *The Great Indian Middle Class*, Penguin Books, New Delhi, 1998.

Venkatachalapathy, A.R., 'Domesticating the Novel: Society and Culture in Inter-war Tamil Nadu', *The Indian Economic and Social History Review*, vol. XXXIV, no. I, January-March 1997.

________, *In Those Days There was No Coffee: Writings in Cultural History*, Yoda Press, New Delhi, 2006.

Vijayasree, C., ed., *Writing the West: Representations from Indian Languages*, Sahitya Akademi, New Delhi, 2004.

Vishwanathan, Gauri, *Masks of Conquest: Literary Study and British Rule in India*, Faber and Faber, London, 1990.

Wahrman, Dror, 'Virtual Representation: Parliamentary Reporting and Languages of Class in the 1790s', *Past and Present* (1992) 136(1).

Walsh, Judith E., *Domesticity in Colonial India: What Women Learned when Men gave them Advice*, Oxford University Press, New Delhi, 2004.

Walton, John K. and James Walvin, ed., *Leisure in Britain: 1780-1939*, Manchester University Press, Manchester, 1983.

Wilensky, H.L., 'Work, Careers and Social Integration', *International Social Science Journal*, vol. 12, 1960.

Wood, Ananda E., *Knowledge Before Printing and After*, Oxford University Press, New Delhi, 1985.

Zachariah, Benjamin 'The Chemistry of a Bengali Life: Acharya / Sir Prafulla Chandra Ray in his Times and Spaces', in Crispin Bates, ed. *Beyond Representation: Colonial and Postcolonial Constructions of Indian Identity*, Oxford University Press, New Delhi, 2006.

(b) *Malayalam*

Amma, Kalamandalam Kalyanikutty, *Mohiniyattam*, National Book Stall, Kottayam, 1978.

Amma, Karthiyanikutty, *Thirumumbinoppam*, Chintha Publishers, Thiruvanthapuram, 2006.

Amma, V. Parukkutty, *K.P Kesava Menon*, Sahitya Akademi, New Delhi, 2005.

Azheekode, Sukumar, *Azheekodinte Athmakadha*, DC Books, Kottayam, 2010.

Balakrishnnan, P.K., *Chandu Menon: Oru Padanam*, D.C. Books, Kottayam, 2006 (1st pub.1957).

Balan, Kantampulli, *Circus*, Sahitya Parishad Cooperative Society Ltd., Ernakulam, 1961.

Bhaskaranunni, P., *Keralam: Irupadhaam Noottandinte Aarambathil*, Kerala Sahitya Akademi, Trichur, 2005.

———, *Pathompadhaam Noottandile Keralam*, Kerala Sahitya Akademi, Trichur, 1988.

Bilathikulam, Jayan, *Veedum Anbathu Varshavum*, The State Institute of Languages, Thiruvanthapuram, 2008.

Champad, Sreedharan, *Circusinte Lokam*, Mathrubhumi Books, Kozhikode, 2008.

Ganesh, K.N., *Keralathinte Innalegal*, Department of Cultural Publications, Thiruvanthapuram, 1997.

Hussain, P. Zakir, ed., *Kozhikode Orormappusthakam*, Olive Publications, Kozhikode, 2012, p.102.

Irumbayam, George, *Malayala Novel Pathonpatham Noottandil*, Department of Cultural Publications, Thiruvanthapuram, 1997.

———, *Naalu Novelukal*, Kerala Sahitya Akademi, Trichur, 1983.

Kumar, A.V. Anil, *Yiramyav: Atimayude Jeevitham*, Mathrubhumi Books, Kozhikode, 2009.

Kunhappa, Murkoth, *Cinema*, The Mangalodayam Ltd., Trichur, 1951.

Moosathu, C.K., *K. Madhavan Nair*, Mathrubhumi, Kozhikode, 1987.

Naduvattam, Gopalakrishnan, *Atmakadha Sahityam Malayalathil*, State Institute of Languages, Thiruvanthapuram, 1985.

Nair, P.C. Sukumaran and P.M. Sudhakaran, eds., *Mathrubhumiyude Charitram*, Mathrubhumi, Calicut, 2000.

Namboodiripad, E.M.S., *Keralam Malayalikalude Mathrubhumi*, Chintha Publishers, Thiruvanthapuram, 2009 (1st pub. 1948).

Narendran, K.M., 'Mrigabalikal Vijayolsavangal', *Mathrubhoomi Weekly*, 25-31 October 1998.

Pazhassi, Prabhakaran., *Sanjayan Kalathinte Manasaakshi*, Department of Cultural Publications, Government of Kerala, Thiruvanthapuram, 2000.

Pottekkatt, S.K., *Ente Vazhiyambalangal*, Poorna Publications, Kozhikode, 2008.

———, *Oru Desathinte Katha*, DC Books, Kottayam, 2006 (1st pub. 1971).

Priyadarshan, G., *Malayala Pathrapravarthanam: Prarambha Swaroopam*, Kerala Sahitya Akademi, Trichur, 1982.

Pulikottil, Anthony., ed., *Sanmargadarshini Vayanasala Platinum Jubilee Smaranika*, 2005.

Raghavan, Puthuppally, *Kerala Patrapravarthana Charitram*, Kerala Sahitya Akademi, Trichur, 1985.

Rajasekharan, K.P., 'Vyavasayika Nagarathinte Randu Nootandu', *City Directory-97*, Calicut Corporation, Calicut, 1997.

Ramachandran, C.K., *Chikilsichum Chirichum*, Malayala Manorama, Kottayam, 2009.

Ravikumar, K.S., *Adyakaala Kathakal*, Current Books, Kottayam, 1993.

Salim, P.B. et al., eds., *Malabar: Paithrukavum Prathapavum*, Mathrubhumi Books, Kozhikode, 2011.

Seluraj, T.B., *Kozhikkodinte Paithrukam*, Mathrubhumi Books, Kozhikode, 2011.

Thalasserry: Sarada Krishnayyar Memorial Fine Arts Society Smaranika, Chitra DTP Solutions, Tellicherry, 2002.

Thirunilath and Joseph, eds., *Kerala Film Directory,* Joseph and Co., Cochin, 1956.

Valsala, P., *Thikkodiyan,* Sahitya Akademi, New Delhi, 2004.

Vijayakrishnan, *Malayala Cinimayude Kadha,* Mathrubhumi Books, Kozhikode, 2004.

Vinayachandran, P., *Kerala Chikilsa Charitram,* Current Books, Kottayam, 2001.

Index